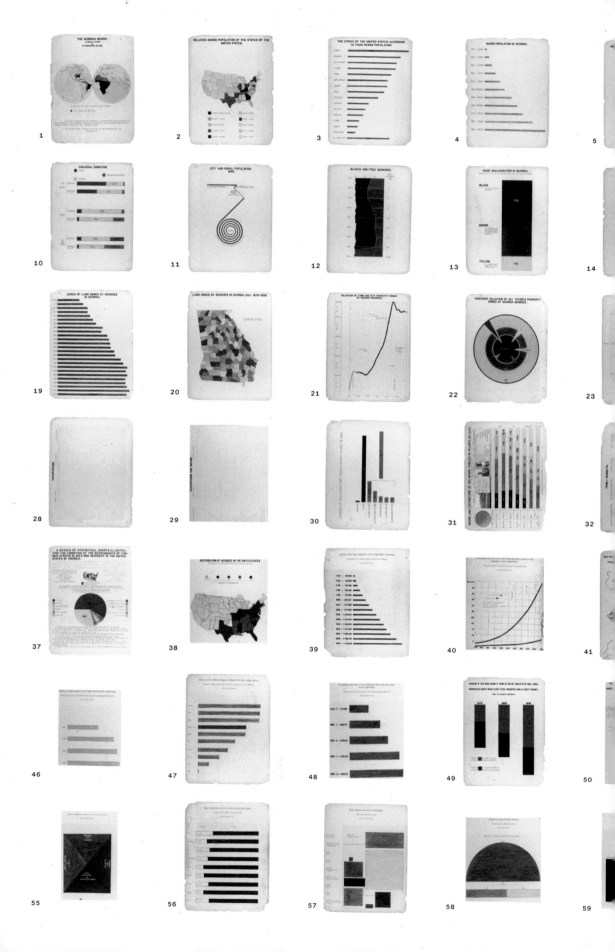

"The problem of the twentieth century
is the problem of the color-line."

—W.E.B. DU BOIS

W. E. B. Du Bois's Data Portraits

Visualizing Black America

THE COLOR LINE AT THE
TURN OF THE TWENTIETH CENTURY

Whitney Battle-Baptiste and Britt Rusert, editors

THE W. E. B. DU BOIS CENTER
AT THE UNIVERSITY OF MASSACHUSETTS AMHERST

PRINCETON ARCHITECTURAL PRESS   NEW YORK

Published by Princeton Architectural Press
202 Warren Street, Hudson, NY 12534
www.papress.com

Image credits:
   Pages 10, 18, 25, 26: W. E. B. Du Bois Papers (MS 312). Special
Collections and University Archives, University of Massachusetts
Amherst Libraries.
   Page 20: Reproduction by permission of the Buffalo & Erie
County Public Library, Buffalo, New York.
   All other images are reprinted courtesy of the Library of Congress,
Prints & Photographs Division.

Editors: Nolan Boomer and Nina Pick   Designer: Benjamin English

Special thanks to: Paula Baver, Janet Behning, Abby Bussel,
Jan Cigliano Hartman, Susan Hershberg, Kristen Hewitt, Lia Hunt,
Valerie Kamen, Jennifer Lippert, Sara McKay, Parker Menzimer,
Eliana Miller, Wes Seeley, Rob Shaeffer, Sara Stemen, Marisa Tesoro,
Paul Wagner, and Joseph Weston of Princeton Architectural Press
—Kevin C. Lippert, publisher

Library of Congress Cataloging-in-Publication Data

Names: Du Bois, W. E. B. (William Edward Burghardt), 1868-1963. |
   Battle-Baptiste, Whitney, editor. | Rusert, Britt, editor.
Title: W.E.B Du Bois's data portraits : visualizing Black America / Whitney
   Battle-Baptiste and Britt Rusert, editors.
Description: First edition. | [Amherst, Mass.] : The W.E.B. Du Bois Center At
   the University of Massachusetts Amherst ; Hudson, N.Y. : Princeton
   Architectural Press, [2018] | Includes bibliographical references.
Identifiers: LCCN 2018007923 | ISBN 9781616897062 (hardcover ; alk. paper)
Subjects: LCSH: Du Bois, W. E. B. (William Edward Burghardt), 1868-1963. |
   African Americans--Social conditions--Charts, diagrams, etc. | Information
   visualization. | Sociology--United States--History. | African American
   sociologists. | Exposition universelle (1900 : Paris, France) | LCGFT:
   Graphs.
Classification: LCC E185.86 .D846 2018 | DDC 323.092--dc23
LC record available at https://lccn.loc.gov/2018007923

Contents

Introduction

Whitney Battle-Baptiste
and Britt Rusert

In his little-known speculative fiction "The Princess Steel" (ca. 1908–10), scholar, writer, and civil rights leader W. E. B. Du Bois weaves a tale about a black sociologist who stages a magnificent experiment on the top floor of a Manhattan skyscraper overlooking Broadway. At the center of this short story stands a *megascope*, a fictive technology that looks like a giant trumpet, laced with "silken cords like coiled electric wire," and equipped with handles, eyepieces, and earpieces. When hooked up to the megascope, users are able to view the "Great Near," Du Bois's term for the always present but usually invisible structures of colonialism and racial capitalism that shape the organization of society. The vision produced by the megascope—a fantastical feudal allegory of primitive accumulation centered on an epic battle between two knights for possession of an African princess whose hair is made of steel—is generated in part by data contained in a massive set of volumes lining

the wall of the laboratory, a vast set of demographic studies collected for over "200 years" by some kind of "Silent Brotherhood." Dr. Hannibal Johnson, the sociologist and protagonist of the story, uses this data to plot what he calls the "Law of Life" onto a "thin transparent film, covered with tiny rectangular lines, and pierced with tiny holes," and stretched over a large frame. He then goes on to plot what he calls "The Curve of Steel" onto a glittering, crystal globe suspended in the air and upon which the megascope's feudal vision subsequently takes shape.[1]

In a story populated by mysterious scientists, annoying lovebirds, towering skyscrapers, battling knights, glimmering treasure, and a regal princess, it's easy to miss that Du Bois's "Silent Brotherhood" likely refers to an actually existing school of black sociology in the US South at the turn of the century, headed by Du Bois himself at Atlanta University.[2] Furthermore, here at the beginning of his pulpy short fiction, Du Bois offers a narrative of what we would today call "data visualization," the rendering of information in a visual format to help communicate data while also generating new patterns and knowledge through the act of visualization itself.

The visual projection of data in Du Bois's sci-fi laboratory would be simply an interesting textual detail were it not for the fact that Du Bois himself had in 1900 contributed approximately sixty data visualizations, or infographics, to an exhibit at the Exposition Universelle in Paris dedicated to the progress made by African Americans since Emancipation. This *Exposition des Nègres d'Amérique* was organized by Thomas Junius Calloway, a lawyer, educator, Fisk University graduate, and editor of the *Colored American* newspaper in Washington, DC, who, with the endorsement and assistance of Booker T. Washington, successfully petitioned the United States government to include, as part of its showcasing of its industrial and imperial prowess as well as its

8

commitment to social reform, an exhibit dedicated to African American life. The American Negro Exhibit featured many contributions by students and faculty at the Tuskegee Institute, Howard University, the Hampton Institute, and other black colleges and industrial schools. The installations that comprised the American Negro Exhibit were meant to educate patrons about the forms of education and uplift occurring at black institutions and in African American communities across the US South. The exhibit featured an eclectic set of objects, images, and texts, including framed photographic portraits of prominent African American leaders and politicians; tools, harnesses, and other agricultural products from black industrial schools; a bronze statuette of Frederick Douglass; and an on-site collection of over two hundred and fifty publications authored by African Americans and compiled by Daniel Alexander Payne Murray, a black intellectual, bibliographer, and librarian at the Library of Congress.

Calloway reached out to W. E. B. Du Bois, his former classmate and friend from Fisk, in the hopes that he would be willing to contribute a social study about African American life to the exhibit. Du Bois used this invitation as an opportunity to contribute two unique sets of data visualizations to the American Negro Exhibit. Heading a team composed of students and alumni from Atlanta University, Du Bois created a collection of graphs, charts, maps, and tables that were generated from a mix of existing records and empirical data that had been collected at Atlanta University by Du Bois's sociological laboratory. Eugene F. Provenzo Jr., author of *W. E. B. Du Bois's Exhibit of American Negroes*, notes that "most of the information for the charts was drawn from sources such as the United States Census, the Atlanta University Reports, and various governmental reports that had been compiled by Du Bois for groups such as the United States Bureau of Labor."[3]

Exposition des Nègres d'Amérique,
Paris Exposition, 1900.

The first set of infographics created for the American Negro Exhibit was part of Du Bois's *The Georgia Negro: A Social Study*, the study he prepared specifically for the Exposition Universelle at the request of Calloway. Representing the largest black population in any US state, Du Bois and his team used Georgia's diverse and growing black population as a case study to demonstrate the progress made by African Americans since the Civil War.[4] In addition to holding up Atlanta University's home state as representative of black populations across the country, Du Bois and his team were interested in establishing the Black South's place within and claim to global modernity.

The second set of infographics prepared by Du Bois and his team at Atlanta University was more national and global in scope. Titled *A Series of Statistical Charts Illustrating the Condition of the Descendants of Former African Slaves Now in Residence in the United States of America*, this set included renderings of national employment and education statistics, the distribution of black populations across the nation, a comparison of literacy rates in the United States relative to other countries, and other striking visualizations. Despite the existence of two separately titled series, important points of cross-reference and connection are visible across both sets of images. For example, the map depicting routes of the African slave trade (see plate 1), which served as the lead image for the Georgia study, situates Georgia (represented by a star) at the center of the map's diasporic cartography, bringing the Georgia study into the orbit of the global scope of the second series while also maintaining its more local orientation.

While scholars have thoroughly explored the American Negro Exhibit, especially the photo albums curated by Du Bois and also exhibited as part of the Georgia study, this is the first time that the data visualizations are collected together in book form and reproduced in full

color.[5] We are particularly thrilled to present this collection of images in 2018, on the occasion of Du Bois's 150th birthday celebration, and in conjunction with the work of the W. E. B. Du Bois Center at the University of Massachusetts Amherst, which also houses the W. E. B. Du Bois Papers. In addition to contributing a new vantage on the history of the American Negro Exhibit and African American participation in world's fairs and expositions, we hope that the infographics might connect to

Class in Calculus.

Fisk University, Nashville, Tennessee, ca. 1899.

other genealogies of black design and data visualization, from the centrality of visual design and format in Harlem Renaissance and Black Arts–era publishing, to the role of abstraction and conceptual aesthetics in black visual art in the twentieth- and twenty-first centuries.[6] Produced at the fin de siècle, the infographics look back to a history of data visualization in the nineteenth century deeply connected to the institution of slavery, and the struggle against it, while looking forward to the forms of data collection and representation that would become central to representations and surveys of Harlem in the twentieth century. Indeed, these images anticipate the forms of "racial abstraction" that would come to define social scientific, visual, and fictional representations of Harlem beginning in the 1920s.[7]

Embedded within the consolidation of the social sciences—including sociology and statistics—in the late nineteenth century, the Du Bois data portraits reflect a moment just before the disciplines had hardened into the academic specializations and structures of knowledge that we are familiar with today. The cross-fertilization of visual art and social science here marks an important transitional moment in the history of the disciplines while offering alternative visions of how social scientific data might be made more accessible to the populations and people from whom such data is collected.

The collaborative nature of work that went into the construction of the images as well as their public exhibition illuminate Du Bois's investment in a truly public sociology. Du Bois also turned to Atlanta alumni to construct a robust network of field researchers across the South. Black women were among the field researchers who contributed their expertise and labor to the Atlanta Studies.[8] We might further speculate on how white working-class patrons touring the American Negro Exhibit in Paris interpreted and made meaning of this data on their own

Atlanta University, Georgia, ca. 1899–1900.

terms. Here, both viewers of the infographics and black study participants in the US South come into view as legitimate co-producers of
sociological knowledge.

The striking aesthetic dimensions of the infographics are further
worthy of reflection and study on their own terms. Indeed, the politics
of visuality, and the very question of black visibility, were central to
Du Bois's thought, and his theory of double consciousness was expressed
in a distinctly visual register.[9] Du Bois used the term "double consciousness" to describe the experience of always seeing oneself through the
eyes of another—a psychic alienation and social isolation produced by
the "peculiar" condition of being black in America. This double or
doubled consciousness was also, according to Du Bois, a kind of "second
sight" that might be transformed from a curse into a "gift" that offered
a unique and superior perspective on turn-of-the century race relations,
sociability, and even existence itself.[10] From his creation of the megascope in "The Princess Steel" to his appeal for a projector to enlarge and
present his sociological data at Atlanta University, Du Bois's thinking
on the politics of the visual also extended to an interest in photography,
film, and other visual technologies, as well as to the politics of access
to these technologies. In addition to the infographics, the Georgia study
also included three photo albums that visually represented the industry,
beauty, and dignity of African Americans in the state. Deborah Willis
notes that Du Bois, working as a compiler and curator of images solicited
from Atlanta photographer Thomas Askew and other black Southern
photographers, "used the camera as a collector of evidence to support
his sociological findings."[11] We invite further reflection on the relationship between the Georgia study photo albums and the fascinating set of
data portraits collected here. These charts, graphs, and maps visualize
African Americans in ways that speak to but also diverge from the

representational strategies used in black uplift photography at the turn of the twentieth century.

Looking back to his years at Atlanta University in his 1968 *Autobiography*, Du Bois wrote that he viewed the contribution of the infographics to the Paris Exposition as an opportunity to display the work of the Atlanta School of sociology to the "thinking world." He goes on to note, "I got a couple of my best students and put a series of facts into charts.... We made a most interesting set of drawings, limned on pasteboard cards about a yard square and mounted on a number of movable standards."[12] In a time when, as chronicled by Aldon Morris, the contributions of the Atlanta Sociological Laboratory were being obfuscated by the Chicago School of sociology, while a broader American culture was not ready to recognize the existence of a school of black sociologists in the US South, Du Bois turned to a visual medium—and the protomodernist aesthetics of turn-of-the-century data visualization—to gain the attention of an international audience.[13] In opposition to the deeply allegorical and intentionally convoluted language that Du Bois deployed in his writings to convey the structures of oppression, alienation, and isolation under Jim Crow segregation—or what Du Bois termed "life within the Veil"—here Du Bois and his design team used clean lines, bright color, and a sparse style to visually convey the American color line to a European audience. This stylistic decision opens up questions about the *aesthetics of the color line* and their relationship to Du Bois's famous proclamation in *The Souls of Black Folk* (1903) that "the problem of the twentieth century is the problem of the color-line" (see also plate 1: *The Georgia Negro: A Social Study*).[14] This focus on modernist design, as well as the diasporic sensibilities of the images, further points to Du Bois's interest in representing the Black South as an integral part of modernity, a "small nation of people" who shared

more in common with the broader, future-oriented "thinking world" than with an insular, backward-looking United States, where Jim Crow segregation was the rule of the land. (See Mabel Wilson's essay for a further exploration of the robust cartographic imaginary of Du Bois's Georgia study.)

Later in his life, Du Bois recalled the contingencies and difficulties that surrounded the completion of this work for the Exposition Universelle, as well as the financial circumstances that nearly prevented him from accompanying his own exhibit:

> The details of finishing these 50 or more charts, in colors, with accuracy, was terribly difficult with little money, limited time and not too much encouragement. I was threatened with nervous prostration before I was done and had little money left to buy passage to Paris, nor was there a cabin left for sale. But the exhibit would fail unless I was there. So at the last moment I bought passage in the steerage and went over and installed the work.[15]

This image of Du Bois traveling across the Atlantic in steerage—in close proximity to the hold of the ship—does not sit comfortably with our own image of Du Bois as a cultural elite and famous intellectual, nor does it reflect the same vision of racial progress and modernity represented in the infographics themselves. We see instead a Du Bois whose own person was less mobile than the graphs and charts sent ahead to Paris; a Du Bois who worked within the financial constraints of a black Southern college and was subject to uneven and precarious grant funding to support his research and travel.

Moreover, although non-white patrons could be more sure of their admittance to expositions in Europe than in the United States, all world's fairs in the period, including the Paris Exposition, were deeply

W. E. B. Du Bois's exhibitor card for
the Paris Exposition, 1900.

invested in visualizing social Darwinist theories of civilization that placed Europeans and Anglo-Americans above non-white peoples; they endorsed a vision of industrialization that equated progress with Anglo-Saxon superiority. While the American Negro Exhibit displayed the positive influence of activism and uplift *within* black communities in the United States, the broader logic of the Exposition, which imagined the white race as lifting up the rest of the world out of barbarism and backwardness, was still an imperial one.

Beyond the material and symbolic constraints posed by what Du Bois would recognize not just as a national but global regime of segregation by the end of World War I, the infographics are also marked by more material reminders of the weighty impress of a history of oppression on Du Bois's present. A short write-up about the Atlanta University contribution to the Exposition Universelle in the *Bulletin of Atlanta University* (1900) includes a brief comment that one of the charts in the exhibit was displayed in a wooden frame carved by a former slave who lived in Atlanta.[16] This elusive and fascinating detail regarding a physical object that has been since lost—a frame designed by an ex-slave—presents us with a stunning juxtaposition that points neither to historical progress nor to the overcoming of the slave past but to the ways that slavery continued to quite literally *frame* the present. Similarly, alongside the Georgia study's data visualizations and photo albums, Du Bois included a three-volume, handwritten compilation of the Black Codes of Georgia, stretching from the slave codes of the colonial and antebellum period to the segregationist policies and laws of the present. In other words, once the data visualizations are contextualized within the broader exhibit and its contents, a much more complicated narrative emerges about the purpose and significations of these images. The presence of Georgia's Black Codes, which sought to control and suppress black

S O U V

PAN-AMERICAN

NEGRO

Souvenir of the American Negro Exhibit at the Pan-American
Exposition in Buffalo, New York, 1901.

ENIR of the

EXPOSITION

XHIBIT

movement and social organization at every turn, ultimately conveyed not a utopian and happy narrative about black progress in a forward-looking, modern nation, but a sense of the gains that had been made by African Americans *in spite of* the machinery of white supremacist culture, policy, and law that surrounded them. In this way, the data portraits actually challenged the dominant framework of liberal freedom and progress that characterized both the American Negro Exhibit and the Paris Exposition.

After the Exposition Universelle closed in November 1900, the entire American Negro Exhibit was packed up, shipped, and displayed at a number of world's fairs and other expositions back in the United States, gaining additional audiences—including African Americans—after its international debut in Paris. For example, a group of black clubwomen worked to bring the exhibit to the Pan-American Exposition in Buffalo, New York, in 1901. It's clear that Du Bois also continued to think about the infographics he and his team prepared for the exhibit. In 1909, he even wrote Calloway to ask how he might secure the return of his exhibit from the Library of Congress, where artifacts and documents from the American Negro Exhibit had been deposited.[17] The current existence of these images as a complete set in the collections of the Library of Congress (all of which have been digitized) suggests that Du Bois was either unable to secure their return or did not follow up with the library. While we can't know what future plans Du Bois had for the infographics, we do know that they might take on a new life today, from inspiring forms of design and art-making connected to social justice work to their traction within digital projects and other initiatives that are, like Du Bois and his collaborators, envisioning how data might be reimagined as a form of accountability and even protest in the age of Black Lives Matter.[18]

American Negro at Paris, 1900

Aldon Morris

By the turn of the twentieth century, the Industrial Revolution had transformed the modern world. Cultural producers from nations around the globe assembled at the 1900 Exposition Universelle in Paris from April to November. Their purpose was to display artifacts signifying great national achievements and provide evidence suggesting even greater accomplishments in the new century. The fair presented a global stage for nations to strut their sense of national pride.

At the turn of the century, portrayals of black people as subhuman, incapable of attaining great material and cultural achievements, were commonplace throughout the western world. Yet, a different view emerged from the American Negro Exhibit at the Exposition. Here, African Americans were displayed in a series of photographs and artifacts as a proud people, dressed in splendor, as accomplished scholars and intellectuals studying the world with as much competence as one

would imagine from students of Plato, Copernicus, Alexander Crummell, and Frederick Douglass. Indeed, African Americans were depicted as students, lawyers, doctors, major inventors, purchasers of property, and warriors against illiteracy, making major contributions on the world stage in the new century. Organizers of the exhibit bestowed nationhood on the recently freed slaves, referring to them as a small "nation within a nation." This designation of a black nation conveyed the idea of a community with its own integrity, intricate culture, and complex social organization. This counterintuitive portrayal stunned throngs of world visitors who had never seen African Americans through this lens. The exhibit violated white thoughts about black people, especially Americans only three decades removed from slavery.

As the twentieth century approached, these ex-slaves found themselves exiled in their own land, where their unpaid slave labor had constructed one of the world's great empires. Rather than benefitting from this bounty, freedmen and -women found themselves homeless, penniless, stripped of the vote, unable to seek education, and patrolled by whites. Indeed, a new racial order was forged. The Jim Crow regime made sure state laws required black subordination in the former Confederacy. In 1896 the United States Supreme Court ruling *Plessy v. Ferguson* legalized Jim Crow rule across the land by declaring racial segregation constitutional so long as segregated facilities were equal. However, whites who never intended to establish equal facilities proceeded to support racial inequality under the guise of legality.

Lacking land, capital, and political rights, ex-slaves, now forced into exploitative relations with former masters, became sharecroppers with no power to benefit from these unequal relations, which predictably resulted in a system of debt peonage. Whites claimed that ex-slaves were the architects of their fate because of racial inferiority; this ideology

W. E. B. Du Bois
at Paris Exposition,
1900.

maintained that blacks were the wretched of the earth because God and nature planned it that way. The disciplines of sociology, anthropology, history, and humanities during Du Bois's time promoted scientific racism. In Du Bois's view, "science" justified this regime of racial exploitation, which in essence was slavery by a new name.

Racial subordination resulted from material powerlessness of the ex-slaves, who had little access to capital and land. African Americans were exploited economically because, despite being forced to provide

Paris Exposition gold medal award,
ca. August 1900.

intensive labor, they depended on meager incomes begrudgingly paid by white elites. Their extreme poverty exacerbated political powerlessness, and their low levels of education provided ideological justification for their servitude.

Although systematically disenfranchised and dispossessed, African Americans mobilized their agency to rebel and pursue economic survival and self-respect. Yet this agency produced by ex-slaves went unacknowledged, denied and disavowed because it conflicted with claims that African Americans naturally belonged at the bottom of the Jim Crow order. Nevertheless, there always existed people acutely aware of their agency and the progress gained during their journey from slavery to freedom. Finally, at the American Negro Exhibit, a narrative of black agency was placed front and center.

Negro Exhibit in Paris, 1900

There was nothing auspicious about the space assigned to the Negro Exhibit, nestled as it was in the right corner of a room in the Pavilion of Social Economy. To garner attention from this unenviable location, this exhibit would need to radiate its own sparkle and originality. It would require an imaginative resonance causing visitors to pause and marvel at the mysteries conveyed by the displays arrayed in the corner. This was no small task given the mission of the exhibit. The American Negro Exhibit successfully captivated thousands of curious visitors over the months it was on display. The exhibit garnered a number of prestigious prizes, including a gold medal awarded to Du Bois by Paris Exposition judges for "his role as 'collaborator' and 'compiler' of materials for the exhibit."[1]

The power of the American Negro Exhibit derived from its sociological imagination.[2] At the turn of the twentieth century, the discipline

of sociology was in its infancy, and its scholars sought to make it a respected social science in America. As a pioneer of scientific sociology in the United States, Du Bois was one of the discipline's leading lights. Du Bois's sociological genius drove the creativity animating the exhibit. Regarding the exhibit's sociological nature, Du Bois explained: "As one enters [the Pavilion of Social Economy], it is an exhibit which, more than most others in the building, is sociological in the larger sense of the term—that is, is an attempt to give, in as systematic and compact a form as possible, the history and present condition of a large group of human beings."[3]

The exhibit's sociological narrative was the result of meticulous planning, on the part of both Du Bois and Thomas Calloway. Calloway explained the goals of the exhibit, writing, "Thousands upon thousands will go [to the fair], and a well selected and prepared exhibit, representing the Negro's development in his churches, his schools, his homes, his farms, his stores, his professions and pursuits in general will attract attention…and do a great and lasting good in convincing thinking people of the possibilities of the Negro."[4]

The sociological content of Calloway's vision was remarkable. He made clear the exhibit would explore crucial aspects of the black American journey, including African American history, intellectual achievements, and advances in education and community building. Calloway was keen on depicting black agency, arguing that the exhibit should demonstrate "what the Negro is doing for himself" through his own organizations. Calloway's sociological imagination reached beyond a narrow focus on African Americans to include "a general sociological study of the racial conditions in the United States"[5] that chronicled and interpreted the social conditions fueling racial inequality. Calloway meticulously examined the materials to be shown in the exhibit and

presented them to faculty and students at Atlanta University in order to receive feedback before they were shipped to Paris. Another African American, Daniel Alexander Payne Murray, played a crucial role in shaping the exhibit. Assistant librarian at the Library of Congress, Murray was a learned man who was an author, intellectual, and expert on black writers and black print cultures, including newspapers, magazines, and pamphlets. Calloway turned to Murray to acquire for the exhibit hundreds of published works by black writers in order to demonstrate black intellectual capacity and achievements in writing.

Du Bois was among the first professors in the nation to train students in sociological theory and empirical methodologies. He involved his students in fieldwork wherein they collected and analyzed data on the black community and race relations. Because these students were taught to think sociologically and engage in data analysis, the most advanced of the group became valuable assistants who compiled charts and graphs. Du Bois's current and former students at Atlanta University were also crucially involved in the development of the exhibit; they worked with him to produce the sociological charts and graphs, doing so on a short timetable. Nevertheless, without Du Bois's direction, training, and sociological imagination, the exhibit would not have blossomed into the masterpiece it became.

Du Bois's Experiences and the 1900 American Negro Exhibit

At the time of the Exposition, Du Bois's experience of living in a racist America prepared him to lead the effort to construct the Atlanta University exhibit. Unlike average members of the black community who grew up under brutal Jim Crow racism in the South, Du Bois began life in

the eastern United States in Great Barrington, Massachusetts. Racism there was subtle and genteel. As a youth, Du Bois did not witness the horrors of lynching and racial violence. Nevertheless, because racism was national in scope, Du Bois first experienced racial discrimination while attending elementary school in Massachusetts. With this first encounter, Du Bois pledged to outperform whites: "Then it dawned upon me with a certain suddenness that I was different from the others, or like, mayhap, in heart and life and longing, but shut from their world by a vast veil. I had thereafter no desire to tear down that veil, to creep through; I held all beyond it in common contempt, and lived above it in a region of blue sky and great wandering shadows. That sky was bluest when I could beat my mates at examination time, or beat them at a footrace, or even beat their stringy heads."[6] Although he experienced discrimination as a child, it was not until he headed to Fisk, a black university in Nashville, Tennessee, that he was faced with extreme prejudice. Entering the land of Jim Crow, which bore striking resemblances to slavery, Du Bois witnessed a virulent, open, and violent racism. It would not take Du Bois long to engage in activism to counter naked racism.

Rather than accept the bombardment of scientific racism, Du Bois launched intellectual and political attacks against it: "When I entered college in 1885, I was supposed to learn there was a new reason for the degradation of the coloured people—that was because they had inferior brains to whites. This I immediately challenged. I knew by experience that my own brains and body were not inferior to the average of my white fellow students. Moreover, I grew suspicious when it became clear that treating Negroes as inferior, whether they were or not was profitable to the people who hired their labor. I early, therefore, started on a personal life crusade to prove Negro equality and to induce Negroes to demand it."[7] In the South, Du Bois had to obey Jim Crow laws and

customs, which applied to all aspects of southern life. He had to ride in the rear of trains where accommodations were filthy and filled with tobacco smoke. He ate meals with blacks and relieved himself in segregated toilets. Despite being a highly educated scholar, the elevated status routinely conferred on similarly situated whites eluded Du Bois. He never adjusted to these racist insults; rather, they often caused him to become angry in five languages. In his crusade to overthrow racism, he developed expertise as a social scientist, historian, philosopher, journalist, novelist, and poet. Du Bois, as he did throughout his life, utilized these talents to develop his contribution to the American Negro Exhibit. Given the talents Du Bois employed to challenge racist views and discrimination, and his dogged persistence, he was able to make inroads on many fronts. In so doing, Du Bois secured his stature as a towering activist of the twentieth century.

Sociological Logic of the Exhibit

Du Bois's own achievements were jarringly inconsistent with the myth of black inferiority. By age twenty, he had earned a bachelor's degree from Fisk University. Three years later, he earned both a bachelor's and master's degree from Harvard. By twenty-five, Du Bois had completed two years of advanced graduate studies at the University of Berlin. At the age of twenty-seven, Du Bois reached a milestone by becoming the first African American to earn a PhD from Harvard. His dissertation, *Suppression of the African Slave-Trade to the United States of America*, became the inaugural volume of Harvard's 1896 series of Historical Studies. Du Bois's 1899 book, *The Philadelphia Negro*, was the first American sociological study of an urban community. At this time, social scientific studies tended to have a social philosophy orientation un-

supported by empirical data. The use of charts and graphs was rare, especially those that were aesthetically pleasing to the eye and the intellect. The achievement of *The Philadelphia Negro* was that it was steeped in empirical data with charts and graphs, which enabled Du Bois to chronicle and analyze the experience of black Philadelphians at the turn of the twentieth century. Du Bois had become one of the most talented sociologists in the nation by the time the idea of a Negro exhibit in Paris took root. However, despite his talent and the innovative nature of his work, white social scientists largely ignored Du Bois's scholarship.

Although subverting scientific racism was a formidable task, Du Bois proceeded undeterred. In keeping with his sociological training at Harvard and Berlin, Du Bois was an astute analyst of the casual forces inhering in social conditions. His expertise included historical, statistical, and comparative analyses, enabling him to unveil the vexing effects of social conditions. Du Bois eschewed ahistorical accounts because he believed that an understanding of people resulted only from examining them in their historical contexts. To understand black people, and their journey from slavery to freedom, required examination with the historical microscope. Du Bois railed against unscientific conclusions based on hearsay and sloppy measurements. His advanced statistical training enabled him to critique and deplore uncritical applications of statistics, especially in studies pertaining to people of African descent. Du Bois pioneered the nation's most sophisticated quantitative research on race and the black population.

The exhibit enabled Du Bois to attack white racist beliefs on a grand stage unavailable in the academy, where white scholars were driven by numerous prejudiced beliefs about African Americans. For instance, by subscribing to the social Darwinist paradigm that theorized the survival of the fittest, white scholars maintained black inferiority would

inevitably lead to the population's extinction. The distinguished white statistician, Frederick Hoffman, declared in 1896, "A combination of these traits and tendencies must in the end cause the extinction of the race."[8] Constructing blacks as a unique race constituted another flaw in studies by white scholars. This belief stemmed from the assumption that people of African descent were not full-fledged members of the human family, which would make comparisons between blacks and whites spurious and unnecessary. Du Bois, who possessed encyclopedic knowledge of social conditions in numerous countries, especially those in Europe, made numerous comparisons between African Americans and Europeans to demonstrate that similarly situated populations acted amazingly similar given shared social conditions. In this sense, Du Bois demonstrated that social conditions trumped race in accounting for social inequality. His contributions to the American Negro Exhibit relied on historical, statistical, and comparative data to challenge the racial stereotypes that were pervasive throughout the academic establishment.

Innovations and Effectiveness of the Exhibit

Du Bois was aware that while unmoving prose and dry presentations of charts and graphs might catch attention from specialists, this approach would not garner notice beyond narrow circles of academics. Such social science was useless to the liberation of oppressed peoples. Breaking from tradition, Du Bois was among the first great American public intellectuals whose reach extended beyond the academy to the masses. Du Bois was able to achieve this feat by using a variety of writing styles ranging from scientific prose to lyrical outpourings across a number of genres that deeply touched readers' emotions. To make their contribution to the American Negro Exhibit captivating, Du Bois and his Atlanta

team decided to produce modern graphs, charts, maps, photographs, and other items that appeared to sparkle. They constructed hand-drawn graphs, charts, and maps arrayed in lively, vibrant colors punctuated by artistically intersecting lines. Bar data contained blocks of contrasting colors documenting the black experience. However, the art did not distract from science; it served to reinforce the comprehensive scientific data chronicling the African American journey. Looking at the images, one is reminded of William Wordsworth's muse: "Dull would he be of soul who could pass by / A sight so touching in its majesty."[9] Indeed an array of dry displays at the exhibit would have been ineffective in subverting the social Darwinist paradigm.

Along with a general approach used to describe the black population nationally, Du Bois employed the case method for his work in the Georgia study. The case method relies on the in-depth study of a single case to reveal details and nuances of phenomena not attainable in a general study. The case method has become commonplace in sociology and anthropology because it allows the analyst to provide specificity to accompany macro-level analysis. Du Bois chose Georgia as a typical state to study African Americans in minute detail in order to add specificity to the national picture; Georgia was an ideal subject because it contained both urban and rural communities and was located close to Atlanta University, where Du Bois's sociological laboratory was housed. Charts, graphs, statistics, and photographs from Georgia accompanied the data visualizations that depicted the United States more generally. Du Bois concluded, "It was a very good idea to supplement these very general figures with a minute social study in a typical Southern State."[10] Together, these methods, art, and analyses generate a powerful sociological narrative of the black experience that ranges in scope from local to international.

The essence of the exhibit's narrative declared that African Americans had made amazing progress over just thirty-five years since Emancipation on most dimensions crucial to human well-being. This progress was remarkable given that black Americans had endured over two centuries of slavery, two decades of Jim Crow, and all the oppressive conditions associated with subjugation. The exhibit suggested that black progress since slavery compared most favorably with that of any human group faced with similar barriers.

Du Bois presented statistical data showing that the black population was increasing rather than decreasing, a direct refutation of social Darwinist theories. Comparative data in the exhibit demonstrated black fertility rates were as robust as that of many European countries. With a slap at the black extinction hypothesis, Du Bois declared, "A comparison of the age distribution with France [shows] the wonderful reproductive powers of the blacks." Du Bois utilized the exhibit to refute the notion that black people were intellectually inferior, uninterested, and incapable of learning. He accomplished this by presenting graphs that showed the black illiteracy rate was rapidly declining and school enrollments were climbing. In graphs comparing black illiteracy rates with those of numerous European countries, Du Bois showed that black "illiteracy is less than that of Russia, and only equal to that of Hungary."[11] The Georgia study also contained hundreds of photographs depicting the physical and social heterogeneity of black people across the Southern state, as well as their dignity. This display of photographs made it difficult to reach any conclusion other than that the people reflected in these images embodied a beauty and grace of their own not describable by white standards of beauty.

The compilation of data displayed at the exhibit stressed one message: black progress since slavery. The colorful hand-drawn illustrations

showed that ownership of black property and land was increasing. Black businesses were rising and so were the number of patents for black inventions. Such inventions overturned the white view that they "never knew a negro to invent anything but lies."[12] Black institutions of higher learning were moving firmly in the direction of educating the race. Other black institutions, including the church and mutual aid organizations, were increasingly fueling black agency. The collection was a masterpiece of sociology, celebrating black humanity on a world stage.

Du Bois was acutely aware that the packaging of the exhibit was as important as the data depicted. He understood what Duke Ellington expressed thirty years later: *It don't mean a thing if it ain't got that swing*. Du Bois and his students, working under a short deadline, analyzed volumes of data before converting them to succinct tables, graphs, and maps. Incredibly, they also mastered the art of drawing numerous illustrations with lively combinations of colors, creative lines, and eye-catching circles. Such visual sociology was rare in these early years of the discipline. In 1900, Du Bois was a pioneer in this form of sociology as he presented the black experience for the world to view at the Paris Exposition. It foreshadowed new possibilities of communicating sociological knowledge to the wider public. From the vantage point of the twenty-first century, the innovative sociology contained in the exhibit continues to stand the test of time.

The Cartography of
W. E. B. Du Bois's Color Line

Mabel O. Wilson

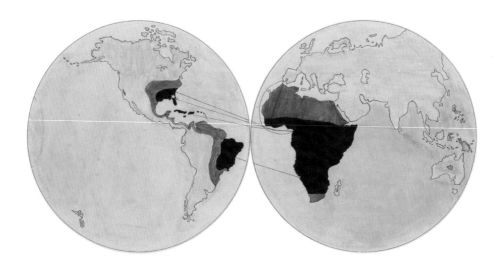

The first plate of W. E. B. Du Bois's *The Georgia Negro: A Social Study* depicts two circles of a globe split in half. In one circle appears Asia, Europe, Africa, and Australia, and in the other North and South America. The plate, hand drawn on a twenty-two-by-twenty-eight-inch sheet of heavy paper, also includes an introductory statement written in neat script: "This case is devoted to a series of charts, maps and other

devices designed to illustrate the development of the American Negro in a single typical state of the United States." That state, Georgia, is located on the map with a star. A gradient of black and brown hues connects the east coasts of North and South America to the west coastline of Africa to demarcate the distribution of the Negro race across the territory of two continents. Five vectors, labeled "routes of the African slave trade," link ports in West Africa to the coasts of Brazil, Santo Domingo, the American South, and Portugal.

This introductory plate of the Georgia study mapped what has come to be called the "Black Atlantic world." It geographically rendered the extent of the African diaspora in the wake of the four-centuries-long transatlantic slave trade that transported an estimated twelve to seventeen million Africans to Europe's colonial holdings in the Americas. Presenting to the primarily white European and American audience visiting Paris's Exposition Universelle, Du Bois gave a visual history lesson on the Atlantic slave trade. With this drawing he promised a scientifically documented report on the current state of black life in Georgia, and speculated on the future of race relations in the United States, announcing at the bottom of the image, "The problem of the twentieth century is the problem of the color-line." In argument with commonly held beliefs among white Europeans and Americans, Du Bois made a compelling case that it was historically constituted racial inequalities—not the Negro's innate moral failings—that would prove a central impediment to black Americans achieving social equality with their fellow white citizens. For Du Bois the legacy of racial castes would stall social, political, and economic advancement in the United States in the new century.

While in Europe to see the exhibit installed in situ at the Paris Exposition, Du Bois joined other American activists, including African American scholar and educator Anna Julia Cooper, in July 1900 at

the First Pan-African Conference hosted at London's Westminster Town Hall. Du Bois charted the international scope of the "color-line" in his speech "To the Nations of the World," delivered to the group dedicated to bolstering Pan-African solidarity and decolonizing the black world. To attendees from across the African continent and the diaspora, the fundamental question of the necessity of Pan-African solidarity could be discerned from, in the words of Du Bois, "how far differences of race— which show themselves chiefly in the color of the skin and the texture of the hair—will hereafter be made the basis of denying to over half the world the right of sharing to utmost ability the opportunities and privileges of modern civilization."[1] Also incorporated into his elegiac *Souls of Black Folk* published three years after the Paris Exposition, these words are perhaps Du Bois's most famous indictment of the centrality of race and racism to modern American sociopolitical life; thirty-five years after Emancipation had legally granted black Americans freedom and citizenship, racism was a wound in the body politic that continued to fester amid widespread racial segregation. His words were clearly meant to also reference the global legacy of the slave trade in depriving black people of their humanity.

How might we, therefore, understand the cartographic, geographic, and historical implications of Du Bois's "color-line" used first in the Georgia study, where it was juxtaposed with a graphic representation of the Black Atlantic world? Throughout the grounds of the nineteenth-century world's fairs, Europeans and Americans put the metropolitan and colonial world on view. Those stories about colonial conquests and magical foreign lands featured in books and newspapers could now be seen firsthand by people strolling through the carefully curated exposition halls, compounds, and grounds. According to scholar Tim Mitchell, "It was not always easy in Paris to tell where the exhibition ended and

39

the world began."[2] Living displays of so-called primitive peoples from the African continent, jungles of South America, and islands of the Pacific could be found at many of the world's fairs. Fair organizers positioned these ethnographic displays in stark contrast to modern progress evident in the myriad of steam engines and industrial goods on view in the machine halls and pavilions. The displays of primitive villages were meant to be both educational and entertaining. The representation of "savage" black and brown peoples affirmed that they lived in a state of nature outside of history, which in turn rationalized the extraction of resources and expropriation of labor from their colonized territories. According to these ethnographic displays, if black Americans had advanced beyond a savage state it was only because of white benevolence and the black adoption of white culture.

It is within this charged context that the infographics debuted in the American Negro Exhibit. The exhibit, which was arranged in an orderly fashion in wooden vitrines that included a system of wing frames displaying multiple formats of information, was located just to the right when visitors entered the pavilion of Social Economy. The two previous Negro Buildings at world's fairs in Atlanta and Charleston, which hosted much larger displays of African American racial progress, had been segregated into separate pavilions, whereas in Paris the American Negro Exhibit was integrated into the larger American display.[3] The contributions to the American exhibit showed maps, diagrams, lantern slides, models, and photographs to demonstrate how new methods in the social sciences were being used to discipline and improve the lives of immigrants, the indigent, children, and African Americans. Calloway placed the visualizations created by Du Bois and his team prominently in the middle of the American Negro Exhibit, where they were mounted on the walls and in the wing frame display boxes.

Through charts and photographs, Du Bois's work provided an empirical study of the various conditions of black life, covering topics such as marriage, mortality, employment, property ownership, education, miscegenation, and various other categories of social progress. One method used for several of these subjects was cartography, which in both sets of infographics spatialized the scale and scope of the black diaspora from the local to the global. Historically, along with the creation of maps—critical tools in the European colonial project—there emerged a cartographic gaze that cultivated a way of seeing the world through evolving cartographic technologies and new modes of representing a world no longer ruled by God and monsters but guided by reason and science. Cartography had given Europeans not only a way of navigating the oceans but also a means of exploring, mapping, and claiming territories in Africa, Asia, and the New World. The desire to map the world brought Europeans in contact with peoples in diverse regions. These colonial encounters recorded in maps and noted in the diaries of explorers provided detailed narratives for natural historians and philosophers to study and invent the comparative physiognomic variations of the human species, leading to geographic-based theories of racial difference. This conceptualization of terrestrial space and time became a productive tool such that, in the words of geographer Denis Cosgrove, "global mapping of climate and physical environments and of biologically defined human groups underpinned geographical theories of race."[4] By linking racial difference to geography and climate, Europeans conceived a teleology of human development that situated themselves as the vanguard of a civilization whose cultural and technological products would be placed on view at the nineteenth-century grand expositions. At the pavilion of Social Economy, conceived by sociologist Ferdinand Le Play, who masterminded the taxonomy of many of the nineteenth-century Paris

fairs, the cartographic gaze was trained on the social landscapes of nations, where modern societies were categorized and subdivided on a hierarchy ranging from those deemed socially undesirable—such as orphans, people of color, and the poor—to those who defined the social norm, such as European and Anglo-American families capable of productively contributing to modern society. The core mission of Du Bois's sociological research was to forcefully refute the widespread belief that black Americans were innately inferior and incapable of social advancement.

In both the Georgia study and the second series of infographics exhibited at the Exposition Universelle, Du Bois and his team redeployed the Western methods of cartography that had been used to marginalize and exploit black life by inscribing the black world back into history and geography. In an essay highlighting the contents of the American Negro Exhibit published in the *American Monthly Review of Reviews*, Du Bois wrote that the entire exhibit recorded black self-determination as a portrait of a "small nation of people" who were "shown to be studying, examining, and thinking of their own progress and prospects."[5] These were bold black-nationalist sentiments—that black Americans could contemplate their past, present, and future connected with an emergent Pan-African solidarity. The black consciousness of a people who understood themselves in a particular time and place strongly refuted the notion that the African had no history, no civilization, and hence no culture. By positioning world history geographically, Georg Wilhelm Friedrich Hegel, in his seminal *Lectures on the Philosophy of History* (1837), observed of Africans that "the condition in which they live is incapable of any development of culture, and their present existence is the same as it has always been. . . . The earliest reports concerning this continent tell us precisely the same, and it has no history in the true

sense of the word."[6] The Du Bois data visualizations, and the American Negro Exhibit as a whole, rebuked beliefs that were foundational to the modern ethos of social progress, particularly the claim that black existence was steeped in what Hegel called "sensuous arbitrariness," that black people lacked the reason and moral capacity to be citizens, poets, philosophers, and a host of other modern subjectivities.

When Du Bois rendered a geographic history of the African slave trade and mapped present conditions in Georgia, he sutured the two together and illustrated through evidence—black lines on white pages—how centuries of racial oppression and exploitation, not a lack of natural aptitude, had shaped the current abysmal conditions of black life worldwide. This was a bold message to broadcast in Paris to a white European and American audience who had been the agents and bene-factors of centuries of ruthless black dispossession. Thus for Du Bois to map the black world was to boldly visualize a cartography refuting Hegel's assertion that "what we understand as Africa proper is that unhistorical and undeveloped land which is still enmeshed in the natural spirit."[7] The series launched a powerful counter-argument, stating that blacks had always been a part of world history and that "black spirit" was evident in the range of culture on view—from literature and poetry to patents and other works of independent black genius. As Du Bois observed, the American Negro Exhibit showed "the development of Negro thought"[8] and revealed "a small nation of people, picturing their life and development, without apology or gloss, and above all made by themselves."[9]

Introduction to the Plates

Silas Munro

A prolific author, renowned sociologist, fierce civil rights advocate, co-founder of the NAACP, and a historian of black lives, W. E. B. Du Bois was also a pioneer of data visualization. The plates that follow are grouped into two distinct but highly related sets. *The Georgia Negro: A Social Study* consists of twenty-nine brightly colored diagrams, plus three maps and four tables. *A Series of Statistical Charts Illustrating the Condition of the Descendants of Former African Slaves Now Resident in the United States of America* includes a group of twenty-seven additional diagrams. Working in ink, gouache watercolor, graphite, and sprinklings of photographic prints, Du Bois and his collaborators at Atlanta University generated crisp, dynamic, and modern graphics as a form of infographic activism. Instead of solely relying on the diorama, a table-top model presentation often used at world's fairs during the time, Du Bois and his team used information design as a rhetorical

45

device.[1] Extant photo documentation shows at least half of the present diagrams mounted in wing frames set on movable standards that allowed fairgoers to flip through large, double-sided plates of the rich data at eye level.[2] Tracing from the slave trade, through the Middle Passage, to Emancipation and beyond, Du Bois's datasets used a unique visual form to make arguments for the equality and sophistication of black Americans living under Jim Crow and the shadow of enslavement.

Made a decade before the rise of dominant European avant-garde movements, these works predate modular design elements often

Detail of plate 31: *Income and Expenditure of 150 Negro Families in Atlanta, GA, U.S.A.*

considered to have their origins in Russian constructivism, De Stijl, and Italian futurism. These modular elements are typically composed of abstract shapes built from circles, triangles, and rectangles in bright primary colors or black and white. The Du Bois infographics were published twenty years before the founding of the Bauhaus, a German art and design school famous for a rigorous foundation, in part focusing on modular design elements. The colors, shapes, and typography of the charts also foreshadow critical developments in the history of data visualization, including simplified pictographic form defined in the Isotype

AMILIES IN ATLANTA, GA., U.S.

ITURE FOR

S.		DIRECT TAXES.	OTHER EXPENSES AND SAVINGS
		THE STATE TAX RATE IS: 1880 – $ 3.50 PER $1,000 1885 – $ 3.50 .. .. 1890 – $ 3.96 .. .. 1895 $ 4.56 .. .. 1899 $5.36 .. .. STATE AND COUNTY TAXES RAISE THIS TO $21 PER $1,000 IN ATLANTA.	THE HIGHER LIFE. RELIGION. ART. EDUCATION. SICKNESS. . SAVINGS. AMUSEMENTS BOOKS AND PAPERS TRAVE

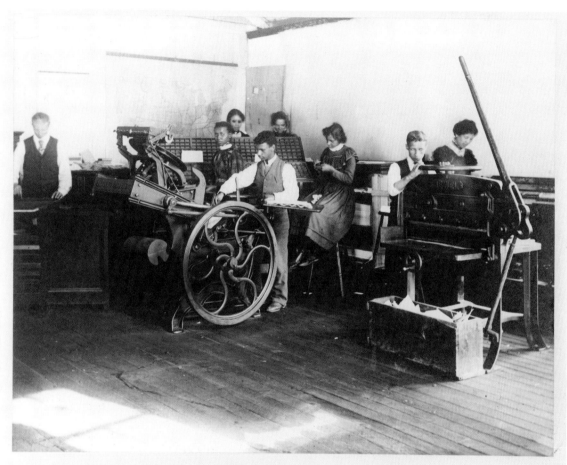

Printing.

Students working printing presses at Claflin University,
Orangeburg, South Carolina, ca. 1899.

picture language, minimal typographic palettes used by the International Typographic Style, and visual narratives in chart form explained in the research of Edward Tufte.[3]

The Georgia study utilizes data gleaned from state census data as well as original research from the department of sociology at Atlanta University, while *A Series of Statistical Charts Illustrating the Condition of the Descendants of Former African Slaves Now in Residence in the United States of America* zooms out to include a wider set of facts and figures on black populations across the United States. Both sets use a range of visual strategies including geographic maps, circle and spiral diagrams, bar and area charts, and complex tables and grids, giving a vivid variety to the data. In multiple instances across the two sets, the Atlanta University team took similar subjects, such as education, colorism, and economic class, and reproduced them twice, with different visual structures. There are considerable differences between the two series of images, including different typographic treatments, level of finish, and consistency of visual language. Yet Du Bois and his team clearly intended a specific reading order to both sets that builds a persuasive narrative through visual data over time.

The diverse chart types show that the Du Bois data portraits are part of a long lineage of visualizing statistical data. The Scottish statistician William Playfair pioneered the bar chart and the line graph (1786), and the pie chart (1801), all of which deeply inform the visual structure of the Du Bois plates.[4] Building on Playfair's work, Florence Nightingale (1820–1910) linked data visualization to social action with her own novel form, the rose diagram (1858), to convince the British government to improve the care of its wounded soldiers.[5] As a well-read and well-traveled intellectual, Du Bois would have had exposure to these and other examples of data in graphic form.

The infographics were the product of multiple forms of collaboration and co-creation. Across the diagrams there are many references to Atlanta University, and the lead infographic of the second series of images explicitly states that it was "prepared and executed by Negro students under the direction of Atlanta University." Contemporary sources suggest that an Atlanta University alumnus, William Andrew Rogers, who had recently received his bachelor's degree in sociology, was the point person responsible for making and coordinating the design and production of the actual graphics.[6] Few records remain about the working methods of Rogers, who may have been living in Petersburg, Virginia, when he worked on the project. Based on the volume of the designs, each piece's complexity and detail, and the compressed project timeline of only a few months to prepare their portion of the American Negro Exhibit, it seems implausible that Rogers and Du Bois worked alone to complete the project.[7] Rogers and Du Bois no doubt facilitated renderings and type-setting from additional unnamed Atlanta University students and alumni, who also assisted with the collection of field data.

Although Du Bois and his team were hardly the first to visualize data with this level of rigor in the pre-computation era, these designs are unique and important. The rhetorical innovation in the social sciences coupled with a visual aesthetic very much at home in the twenty-first century makes for a prescient body of design work. These visualizations offer a prototype of design practices that were not widely utilized until more than a century later, anticipating the trends—now vital in our contemporary world—of design for social innovation, data visualization in service to social justice, and the decolonization of pedagogy.

Plates

Part I
The Georgia Negro:
A Social Study

*All boards are approximately
22 × 28 inches, rendered
in ink and watercolor, unless
otherwise noted.*[8]

Plate 1   W. E. B. Du Bois and his students open the visualizations with a striking map that captures the sweeping nature of their study. Two circles connected by fine lines connect dark areas of Africa to equally dark swaths in the United States, the Caribbean, and South America. A solitary white star represents Georgia in a wave of black ink. Though absent in the key, the gray zones suggest the migration of slaves beyond the most trafficked regions. Here and in many of the subsequent plates, the diagram is larger in scale than the text, while the written rhetoric matches the heaviness of its subject matter. This complex combination of text and image allows Du Bois to visually represent hundreds of years and thousands of miles of oppression.

THE GEORGIA NEGRO.
A SOCIAL STUDY
BY
W.E. BURGHARDT DU BOIS.

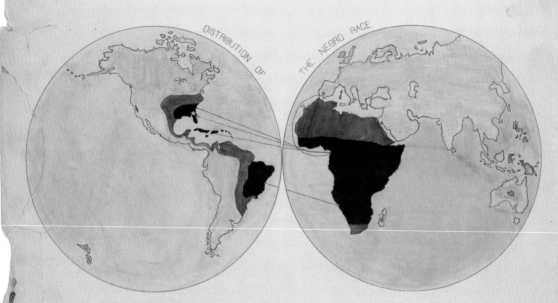

DISTRIBUTION OF THE NEGRO RACE.

≡ ROUTES OF THE AFRICAN SLAVE TRADE.

⊛ THE STATE OF GEORGIA.

THIS CASE IS DEVOTED TO A SERIES OF CHARTS, MAPS AND OTHER DEVICES DESIGNED TO ILLUSTRATE THE DEVELOPMENT OF THE AMERICAN NEGRO IN A SINGLE TYPICAL STATE OF THE UNITED STATES.

" THE PROBLEM OF THE 20TH CENTURY IS THE PROBLEM OF THE COLOR-LINE."

Plate 2   Du Bois and his team are masters of progressive disclosure, a technique that gradually reveals to the viewer the ideal amount of information in each data portrait.[9] Moving from a global scale to a national one, this map of the United States contributes more detail to the previous plate's mapping of the Black Atlantic world (see plate 1). A palette of bright primary colors, complementing subtle shades, and intricate textures conveys a range of black populations at a quick glance. An even more precise breakdown of population continues at the state and county levels in the subsequent charts (plates 3–6).

RELATIVE NEGRO POPULATION OF THE STATES OF THE UNITED STATES.

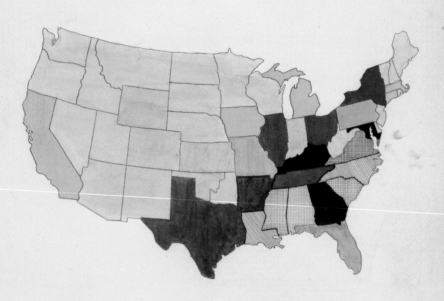

 750,000 NEGROES AND OVER

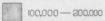 100,000 — 200,000

600,000 — 750,000

50,000 — 100,000

500,000 — 600,000

25,000 — 50,000

300,000 — 500,000

10,000 — 25,000

200,000 — 300,000

UNDER — 10,000

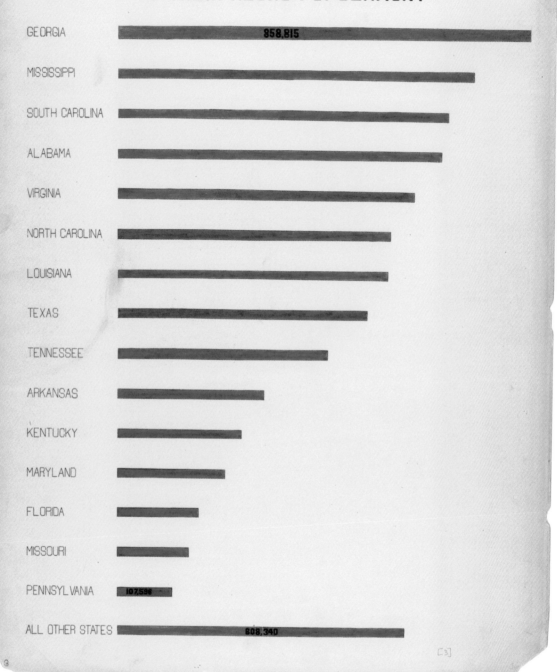

THE STATES OF THE UNITED STATES ACCORDING TO THEIR NEGRO POPULATION.

State	
GEORGIA	858,815
MISSISSIPPI	
SOUTH CAROLINA	
ALABAMA	
VIRGINIA	
NORTH CAROLINA	
LOUISIANA	
TEXAS	
TENNESSEE	
ARKANSAS	
KENTUCKY	
MARYLAND	
FLORIDA	
MISSOURI	
PENNSYLVANIA	107,596
ALL OTHER STATES	608,340

Plate 3 The first bar chart in the series is an expert example of a visual economy of means. The horizontal red bars represent the relative Negro population of the United States broken down by state. The bars are stacked in descending order by population. The only anomaly in the progression appears at the end, where a combined bar at the base captures the remaining states. The most and least populous states are labeled with numerical figures to help viewers estimate the states in between (see plate 19).

NEGRO POPULATION OF GEORGIA.

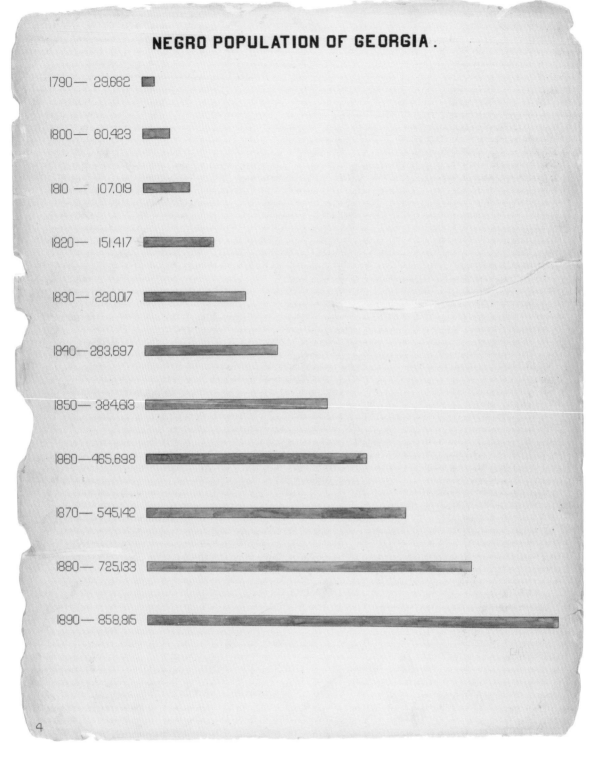

1790— 29,662

1800— 60,423

1810 — 107,019

1820— 151,417

1830— 220,017

1840—283,697

1850— 384,613

1860—465,698

1870— 545,142

1880— 725,133

1890— 858,815

4

Plate 4 Stark black typography and slender rectangles washed in gray record a century of Negro population growth down the blank expanse of the page. This monochromatic bar graph is one of a handful of boards that are free of bright color. The monochromatic color is assigned to this more detailed level of data and matches the black rendering of Georgia in plate 2. The data is shown with simplicity, allowing the viewer a moment of quiet comprehension between more exuberant constructions of information and color in other charts.

NEGRO POPULATION OF GEORGIA BY COUNTIES.
1890.

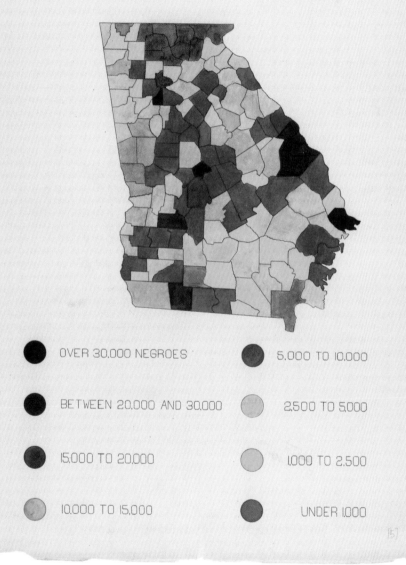

OVER 30,000 NEGROES

BETWEEN 20,000 AND 30,000

15,000 TO 20,000

10,000 TO 15,000

5,000 TO 10,000

2,500 TO 5,000

1,000 TO 2,500

UNDER 1,000

[5]

Plate 5 Many of the diagrams are sequenced strategically to build comparisons and new perspectives on the study's datasets by considering relationships over time as well as space. This population index of *Georgia by Counties, 1890* precedes the following map (plate 6), which shows the populations in 1870 and 1880. The vibrancy and opacity of the colors suggest the use of gouache, a subtype of watercolor that lies down with an opaque finish and bonds with its paper background. This material would later be critical to the flat and graphic visual language taught by the so-called Swiss schools in 1950s and 1960s Europe and spread throughout American graphic design education, especially via Armin Hoffman and his former students from the Basel School of Design.[10]

NEGRO POPULATION OF GEORGIA BY COUNTIES.

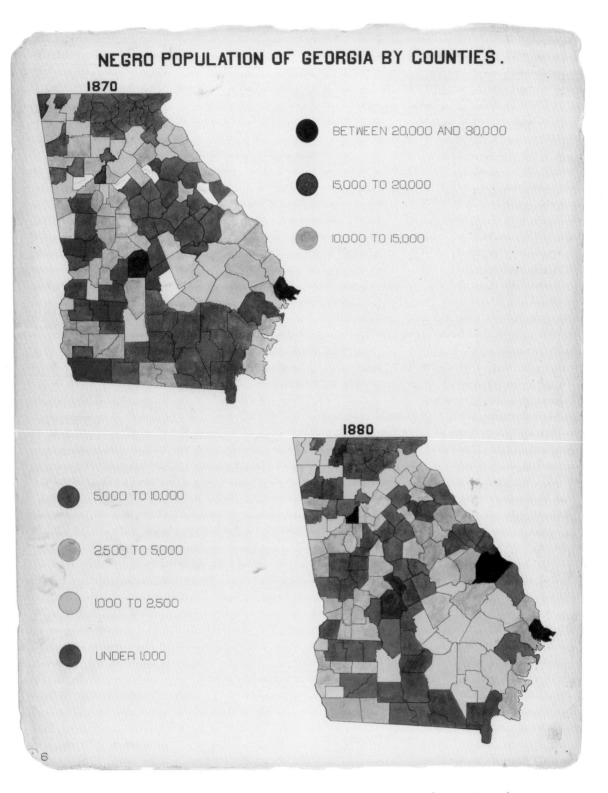

1870

BETWEEN 20,000 AND 30,000

15,000 TO 20,000

10,000 TO 15,000

5,000 TO 10,000

2,500 TO 5,000

1,000 TO 2,500

UNDER 1,000

1880

Plate 6   The pair of state maps rendered here are an early example of a type of diagram taken for granted today: the heat map. Heat maps use color to allow a user to quickly identify highly active, dense, or concentrated parts of a space. First coined and trademarked in 1993 by Cormac Kinney, an enterprising software engineer, the heat map was a tool that used concentrations of color to represent wild swings in stock and mutual fund trading activity.[11] Here, instead of marking the flow of funds, Du Bois maps the density of black Georgians across the state's counties.

Plate 7 Highly detailed and drawn with precision, this line chart tracks the rate of population growth for both whites and blacks in Georgia over the course of a century. The black lines of the growth rates and the red lines of the grid are too fine to be drawn with an ink brush. These delicate marks were likely drawn with a stylographic pen. Stylo pens featured a metal tip embedded with a fine wire to regulate a steady flow of ink and were a popular precursor to the nibbed fountain pen.[12]

COMPARATIVE INCREASE OF WHITE AND COLORED POPULATION OF GEORGIA.

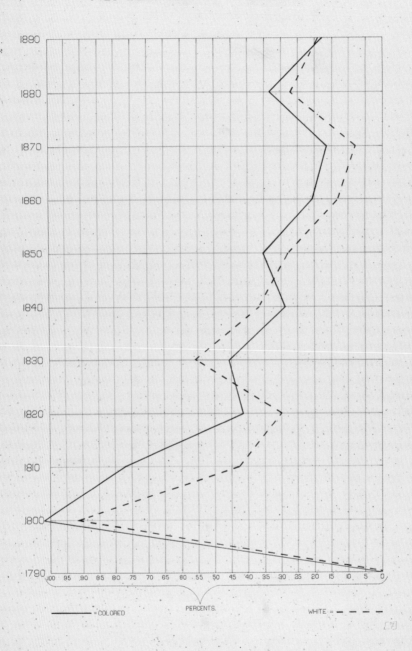

———— = COLORED   PERCENTS.   WHITE = – – – –

Plate 8   Two multicolored maps of the United States vibrate with a rainbow of states rendered in blocks of solid hues, tints, and shades. Only the state of Georgia stands in a rich black with stark type to emphasize its importance in the study. Every other state is overlaid with numerical indices that notate the movement of African Americans between states. Delicate arrows document patterns of migration away from former slave states and anticipate the magnetism of progressive urban cores to blacks in the later Great Migration.

MIGRATION OF NEGROES.
1890.

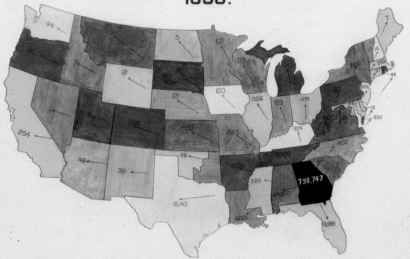

PRESENT DWELLING PLACE OF NEGROES BORN IN GEORGIA.

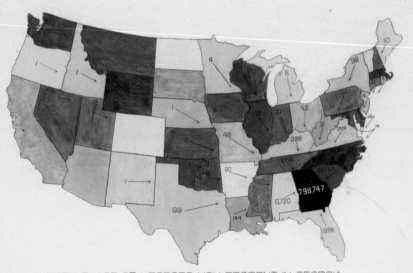

BIRTH PLACE OF NEGROES NOW RESIDENT IN GEORGIA.

[5]

AGE DISTRIBUTION OF GEORGIA NEGROES COMPARED WITH FRANCE.

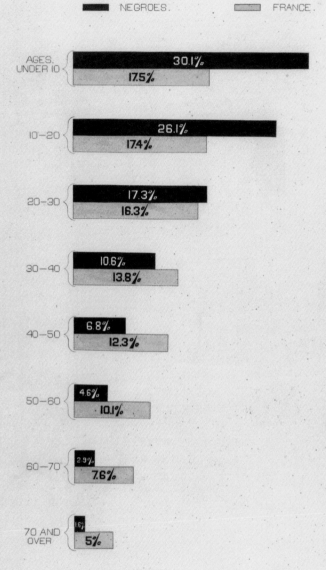

■ NEGROES.　　　▨ FRANCE.

AGES. UNDER 10 — 30.1% / 17.5%

10—20 — 26.1% / 17.4%

20—30 — 17.3% / 16.3%

30—40 — 10.6% / 13.8%

40—50 — 6.8% / 12.3%

50—60 — 4.6% / 10.1%

60—70 — 2.9% / 7.6%

70 AND OVER — 1.6% / 5%

Plate 9 In this chart, Du Bois and his team choose to render data that could connect with an international audience. This straightforward yellow and black bar graph compares the ages of black Americans with their French equivalents of all races. Of particular note are the unique percentage signs that visually outweigh their numerical companions. These glyphs were likely improvised because standard alphabetic characters are not included in the engineered letter template that is the source of most of the typography in the Georgia study.[13] Age ranges are linked to the bar charts with delicate and precise curving braces. The placement of Europeans and Georgia Negroes side by side using comparative data demonstrates the global status and robustness of the African American population.

CONJUGAL CONDITION.

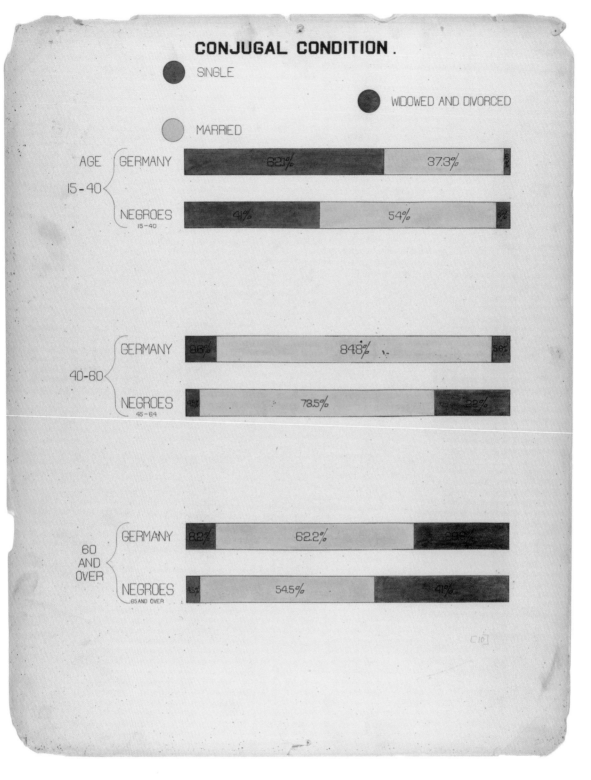

● SINGLE

● WIDOWED AND DIVORCED

● MARRIED

AGE 15-40
- GERMANY: 62.1% / 37.3% / .6%
- NEGROES 15-40: 41% / 54% / 5%

40-60
- GERMANY: 9.6% / 84.8% / 5.6%
- NEGROES 45-64: 4.5% / 73.5% / 22%

60 AND OVER
- GERMANY: 8.2% / 62.2% / 29.6%
- NEGROES 65 AND OVER: 4.5% / 54.5% / 41%

Plate 10 This tricolor chart stacks three pairs of bars representing Germans and black Americans of different marital statuses: red sections for single, yellow for married, and green for widowed or divorced. These are then divided according to designated age ranges. Du Bois chooses Germany, a neighboring presenter at the Paris Exposition, as a point of comparison in order to elevate the status of black Americans in the eyes of audiences abroad and at home. He does this by building a graphic relationship between African American populations and the mainly white populations of a major European power.

Plate 11 Part bar chart, part line chart, and part spiral graph, this visualization defies categorization. The text paired with each segment reads more like a narrative than a typical key. Its primary color palette and fragmentary construction make for a memorable, and experimental, presentation of data.

CITY AND RURAL POPULATION.
1890.

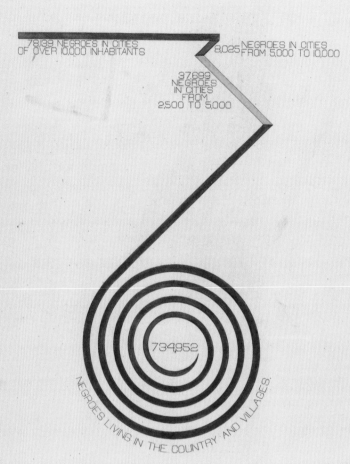

78,139 NEGROES IN CITIES OF OVER 10,000 INHABITANTS

8,025 NEGROES IN CITIES FROM 5,000 TO 10,000

37,699 NEGROES IN CITIES FROM 2,500 TO 5,000

734,952

NEGROES LIVING IN THE COUNTRY AND VILLAGES.

SLAVES AND FREE NEGROES.

	PERCENT OF FREE NEGROES
1790	1.3 %
1800	1.7
1810	1.7
1820	1.2
1830	0.8
1840	0.9
1850	0.7
1860	0.8
1870	100 %

Plate 12 Reading chronologically from top to bottom, this area chart mixes sharp and deckled edges. On the left, a torn black color field shows enslaved Georgians from 1790 to 1890. On the right, a geometrically sculpted red field charts the rise, decline, and rise again of the percentage of free blacks. A simply worded title tops the tensely arranged visual for maximum impact.

RACE AMALGAMATION IN GEORGIA .

BASED ON A STUDY OF 40,000 INDIVIDUALS OF NEGRO DESCENT.

BLACK.
I.E. FULL—BLOODED.
NEGROES.

44%

BROWN.
I.E. PERSONS WITH
SOME WHITE BLOOD
OR DESCENDANTS
OF LIGHT COLORED
AFRICANS.

YELLOW.
I.E. PERSONS WITH
MORE WHITE THAN
NEGRO BLOOD.

16%

Plate 13 The Georgia study also captures the relationship between class and skin tone within black culture. As a free, Northern-born, globally educated, and internationally traveled scholar working at a historically black college in the South, Du Bois had deep personal and empirical experience with what we now know as colorism.[14] The chart shows three categories of race: "black" or "full-blooded Negroes," "brown" or "persons with some white blood or descendants of light colored Africans," and "yellow" or "persons with more white than Negro blood." Rendered in corresponding black, brown, and yellow gouache, the heaviness of this subject is given visceral form. The red "40%" recalls the word *blood* and its usage as a descriptor of race.

Plate 14 This black-and-white bar diagram takes on a very atypical woven structure. Used here for illiteracy figures and their corresponding years, this lattice-like arrangement is repeated in another bar chart about Negro property (plate 23). This repeated style reflects both a necessity to be efficient and the continued exploration that comes with experimentation in an unfamiliar medium. The interleaved bars also visually relate to other curving and turning bar and spiral charts. Both are examples of a tension between Du Bois's interest in condensing data into the most economic form and his leadership of a team of sociologists acting as designers-in-training. Another atypical choice by the Atlanta University team is the representation of extrapolated data not yet measured in their study. Here they postulate an illiteracy rate of 50 percent in 1900 marked with a pair of question marks.

ILLITERACY.

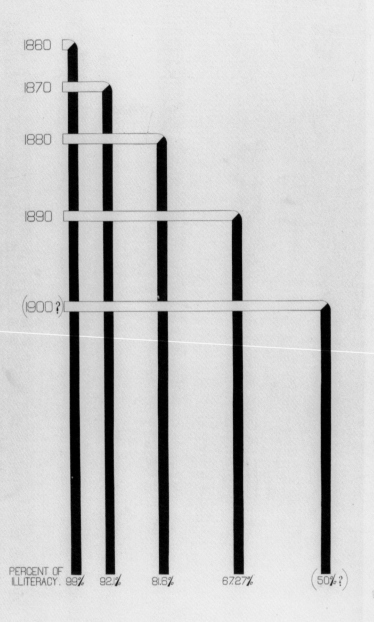

1860

1870

1880

1890

(1900?)

PERCENT OF
ILLITERACY. 99%   92.1%   81.6%   67.27%   (50%?)

[14]

NEGRO CHILDREN ENROLLED
IN THE PUBLIC SCHOOLS .

<u>1860</u>
7

1870

10,351

1878

72,655

1884

110,150

1888

120,533

1891

156,836

1897

180,565

[15]

14

Plate 15 A small array of bars shows the
increasing enrollment of black students in Georgia
public schools. Starting with the sliver of seven
students in 1860—three years before the Emancipation Proclamation—the enrollment rates increase
exponentially before slowing to a more gradual
increase in 1897. The sober presentation of this
information enhances its impact through minimal
visual means.

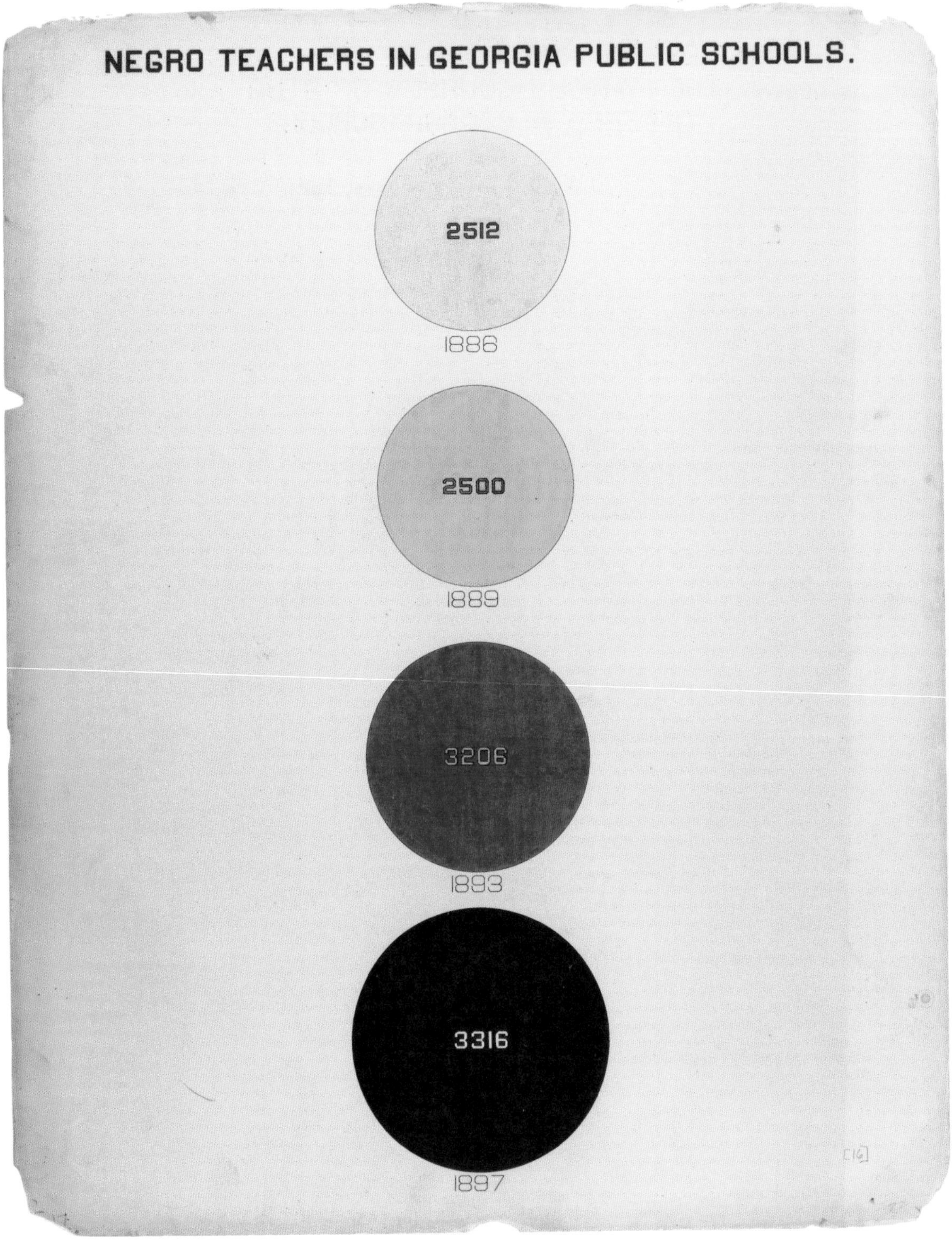

NEGRO TEACHERS IN GEORGIA PUBLIC SCHOOLS.

2512

1886

2500

1889

3206

1893

3316

1897

Plate 16 No chart in the entire set is as graphically simple as this one: four monochromatic circles float in a solitary column, each slightly larger than the previous one. There is no key, just two sets of numbers. The number below the circle represents the year that the data was measured, and the number inside the circle represents the number of black teachers in Georgia public schools that year. This is one of three rare moments in the infographics when both the shape and the typography appear in color. The overall result reinforces the designers' interest in representing an exhaustive amount of information in an efficient and elegant way.

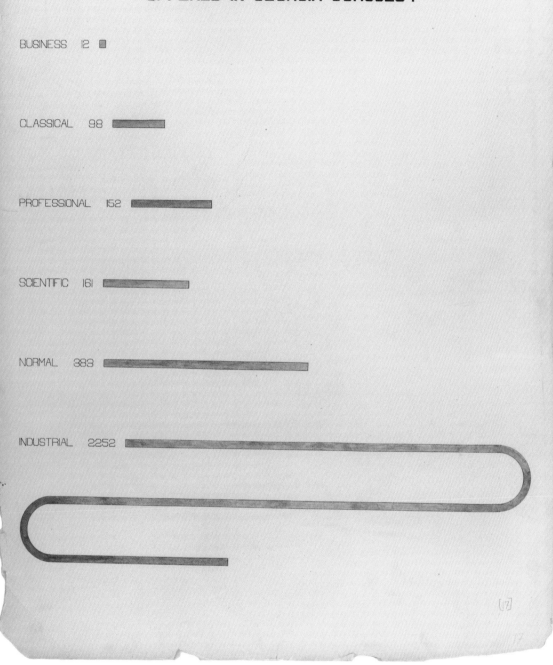

NUMBER OF NEGRO STUDENTS TAKING THE VARIOUS COURSES OF STUDY OFFERED IN GEORGIA SCHOOLS.

BUSINESS 12

CLASSICAL 98

PROFESSIONAL 152

SCIENTIFIC 161

NORMAL 383

INDUSTRIAL 2252

Plate 17 A double-curved outlier at the end of a series of straight bars is a more creative way to show the dramatic ratio of Negro students studying industrial arts. The snaking data is a visual focal point on a chart that shows the dominance of industrial education for black Americans in 1900.

VALUE OF LAND OWNED BY GEORGIA NEGROES.

Plate 18 Eschewing their penchant for geometric shapes, the Atlanta University team created a pictographic hybrid to represent land held by black Georgians. Stylized drawings of burlap sacks are lined up and down the board. Labeled with a year and dollar amount, it is easy to imagine each filled with stacks of United States currency. This iconographic approach is a precedent to the visual language that would surface two decades later when Otto Neurath, Marie Neurath, and Gerd Arntz created the Isotype picture language.[15] Like the Isotype team, Du Bois worked collectively with others and believed that a symbolic visual language could have universal social impact.

ACRES OF LAND OWNED BY NEGROES IN GEORGIA.

Year	
1874	338,769
1875	
1876	
1877	
1878	
1879	
1880	
1882	
1883	
1884	
1885	
1886	
1887	
1888	
1889	
1890	
1891	
1892	
1893	
1894	
1895	
1896	
1897	
1898	
1899	1,062,223

Plate 19 Du Bois and his team generated the greatest number of charts using the bar format. The team was likely familiar with William Playfair, the originator of this diagram type and a statistician who understood the power of the visual. Its rectilinear form and linear structure are easy for the viewer to cognitively process. Its simple style also makes it a natural choice for a team working under time constraints. The arrangement of bars approximates the shape of the state of Georgia itself and, in this way, links to the next image in the series, a map titled *Land Owned by Negroes in Georgia, U.S.A., 1870–1900*.

LAND OWNED BY NEGROES IN GEORGIA, U.S.A. 1870-1900.

THE FIGURES INDICATE THE NUMBER OF ACRES OWNED IN EACH COUNTY IN 1899.

[20]

Plate 20 This map is distinct from the other geographic maps because of its spare form and succinct communication methods. There is no key and almost no typography beyond the title and a short sentence explaining that the numbers represent acres of land held by Georgia blacks. Deep in the map is a small fragment of constructed type paired with a circular symbol representing the city of Macon and a hand-drawn equivalent for the capital, Atlanta.

Plate 21   What appears to be another straight-forward line chart is one of the most overtly political charts in the Georgia study. An undulating black line shows extrapolated property values in outline and actual property values in solid black crossing a red grid of squares. Tucked into the grid is a series of disquieting socioeconomic and political trends: the rise of the Ku Klux Klan and political unrest in the 1870s; new industrialism in the 1880s; followed by lynching, financial panic, disenfranchisement, and proscriptive laws in the 1890s. This diagram powerfully links the economic progress of black Georgians to larger regimes of violence against African Americans, pointing to the widespread disenfranchisement and dispossession of black people in the post-Reconstruction era.

VALUATION OF TOWN AND CITY PROPERTY OWNED
BY GEORGIA NEGROES.

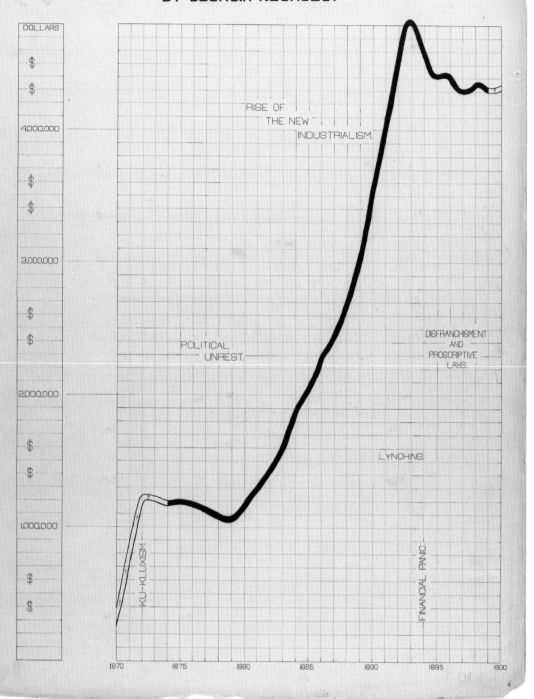

Plate 22   Like a bull's-eye used in target practice, this nested circle chart draws the viewer to dead center. The value of all black-owned land in Georgia in 1875—$5,393,885—appears to float in crisp, white engineered numbers. Rogers, Du Bois, and their team strategically use color and shape to create an optical gravity. As the rings move inward, the value of the colors grows continually darker, with the exception of the one red rim holding the structure together. The eye is drawn in with sharp triangular arrows to the total value of land owned in five-year periods from 1880 to 1889. The arrows are unusually rendered with a pattern of tiny undulations that resemble waves. What looks at first glance like the accidentally shaky hand of a novice production designer is actually an intentional set of wave textures. The circles, triangles, and square of the page anticipate Kandinsky's famous Bauhaus color and shape tests administered to his students decades later.[16] The unusual slicing in this pie chart also evokes Florence Nightingale's polar diagrams from four decades prior.[17]

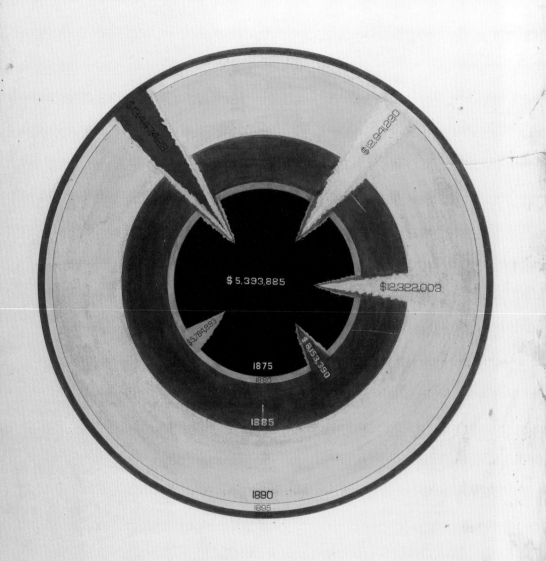

$13,447,423

$12,941,230

$ 5.393,885

$12,322,003

$5,764,293

$ 6,153,390

1875

1880

1885

1890

1895

NEGRO PROPERTY IN TWO CITIES
OF GEORGIA.

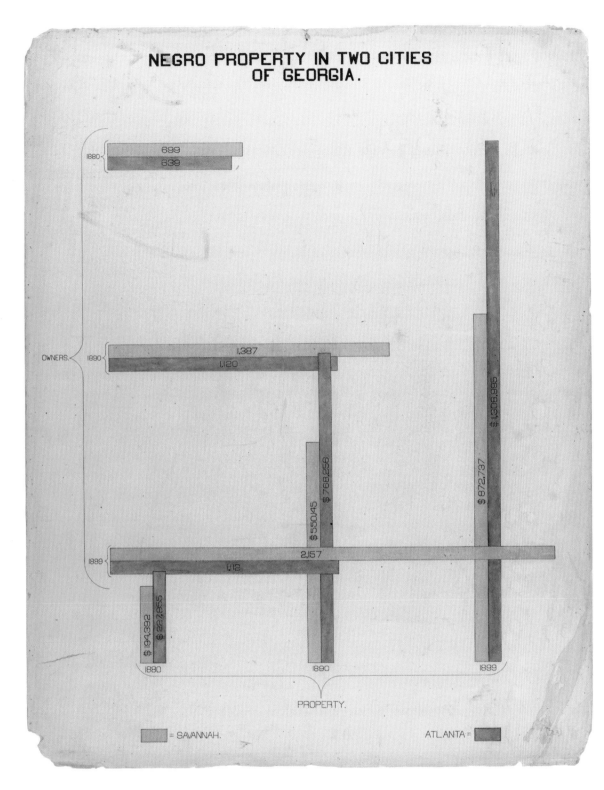

Plate 23 An overlapping matrix of baby blue and yellow bars represents the number of black property owners and land values in two Georgia cities: Atlanta and Savannah. In this carefully woven bar chart, the Du Bois team uses two different data sets to visually reinforce both. As a statistician, Du Bois would be interested in ways to display correlation and even causality in data gathered in different parts of the state in different years. Much like the spiral diagrams before it, this lattice bar chart might be considered its own chart typology: the woven bar chart.

VALUE OF FARMING TOOLS.

1879 ▬▬▬▬▬

1883 ▬▬▬▬▬▬▬

1888 ▬▬▬▬▬▬▬▬▬

1893 ▬▬▬▬▬▬▬▬▬▬▬▬▬▬▬

1898 ▬▬▬▬▬▬▬▬▬▬▬▬▬

Plate 24 Because of the importance of agricultural labor for African Americans in this period, the value of their farm tools was critical. This horizontal stack of brown-colored bands is only identified by the year of value recorded. The choice to leave out the dollar amounts of these figures could be a combination of the expediency of the project and their relatively small value in comparison with other relevant figures such as the cost of property and land.

Plate 25 Six curving bars of color initiate from a stacked block of text listing the value of house- hold furniture owned by black Georgians over a twenty-five-year period. Each spiral is a different pastel or primary color that wraps around a core origin point. The rings show a growing trend over time, each longer than the previous one. The unusual and complex configuration of the spiral diagram here builds on graphic constructions such as Playfair's pie chart and Nightingale's rose diagram. The end result is simultaneously easy to read and hypnotic.

ASSESSED VALUE OF HOUSEHOLD AND KITCHEN FURNITURE OWNED BY GEORGIA NEGROES.

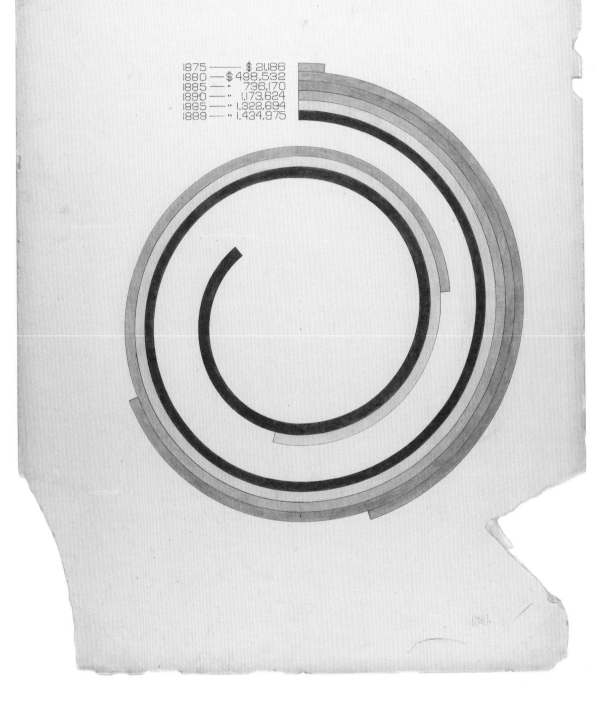

1875 ————	$ 21,186
1880 —	$ 498,532
1885 — "	736,170
1890 — "	1,173,624
1895 — "	1,322,694
1899 — "	1,434,975

Plate 26   This chart documents black male workers in the year 1890. It is uncannily similar to the chart *Occupations in Which 10,000 or More American Negroes are Engaged* (plate 45) in the second study and appears to be a more preparatory diagram focusing on black youth and men over ten years old. Notably, the chart leaves out labor roles predominated by black women, including seamstresses, laundresses, and domestic servants. The top group of agricultural laborers uses one of Du Bois's distinctive curved bars to keep the largest number of workers in proportion without leaving the page. This detail, along with the bold "1890" placed in the middle of the page, suggests that this is an earlier draft of the more refined plate that follows (plate 27).

OCCUPATIONS OF GEORGIA NEGROES.

MALES OVER 10.

Occupation	Count
AGRICULTURAL LABORERS	98,400
FARMERS AND PLANTERS	63,012
LABORERS	29,723
STEAM RAILWAY EMPLOYES	7,440
SERVANTS	7,000
DRAYMEN, HACKMEN	4,390
CARPENTERS AND JOINERS	3,761
SAW AND PLANING MILL EMPOYES	2,471
MESSENGERS	1,970
WOOD CHOPPERS	1,399
BLACKSMITHS AND WHEELWRIGHTS	1,328
CLERGYMEN	1,277
MASONS	1,243
BRICK-MAKERS AND POTTERS	977
BARBERS	899
MERCHANTS	837
PAINTERS, GLAZIERS AND VARNISHERS	676
BOOT AND SHOE MAKERS	632
PROFESSORS AND TEACHERS	620
LIVERY STABLE KEEPERS	620
ENGINEERS	520
GARDNERS AND FLORISTS	519

1890.

OCCUPATIONS OF NEGROES AND WHITES IN GEORGIA.

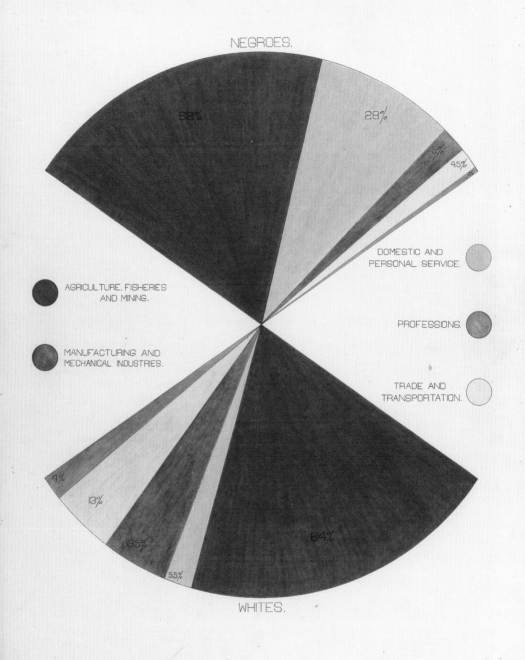

NEGROES.

62%

28%

5%

4.5%

DOMESTIC AND
PERSONAL SERVICE.

AGRICULTURE, FISHERIES
AND MINING.

PROFESSIONS.

MANUFACTURING AND
MECHANICAL INDUSTRIES.

TRADE AND
TRANSPORTATION.

4%

13%

13.5%

5.5%

64%

WHITES.

Plate 27 This circle chart is one of the most visually economical designs in the Georgia study.[18] Radially sliced wedges are filled with a primary color palette that is accented with a light brown and beige that may refer to skin tones. Two sets of larger wedges representing Negroes and whites hover cantilevered at the chart's center point. Du Bois builds dynamic tension by cascading color around the chart in opposing clockwise and counterclockwise directions, making the diagram look as if the "Negro" wedges might collapse over the "White" wedges at any moment. In a feat of spatial economy and visual wit, the key made of intact circles is tucked within the negative space, both echoing and stabilizing the overall composition.

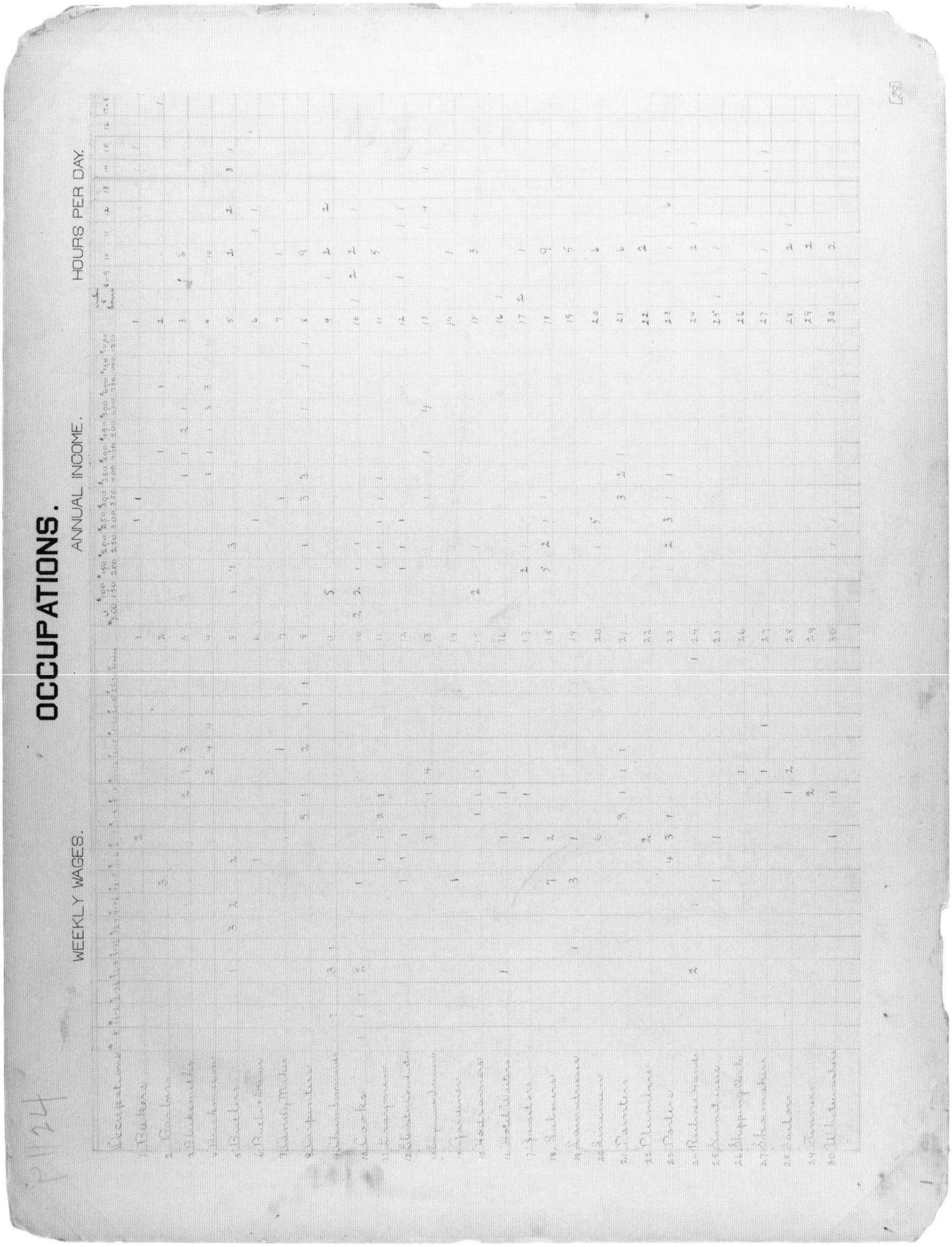

OCCUPATIONS.

WEEKLY WAGES.   ANNUAL INCOME.   HOURS PER DAY.

Plate 28 This table listing occupations and related wages is drawn in graphite. The casual aesthetic coupled with handwritten text suggests that this visualization was created earlier in support of the pie chart that comes before it (plate 27).

OCCUPATIONS AND INCOME.

WAGES BY SEX.

INCOME BY FAMILIES.

OCCUPATIONS BY SEX.

Plate 29 This additional table of black occupations and income was drawn on the reverse of the previous table. This table could hold as much information as other chart types, but much of the grid is composed of empty units drawn in faint pencil. The in-process nature of these and similar boards raises questions about their creation: Were there other preparatory materials that Du Bois, Rogers, and the team used to build the diagrams? Were there multiple teams at work that executed the differing lettering styles, color palettes, and visual structures? What did Du Bois and his team plan for the boards after their exhibition in Paris and across the United States?

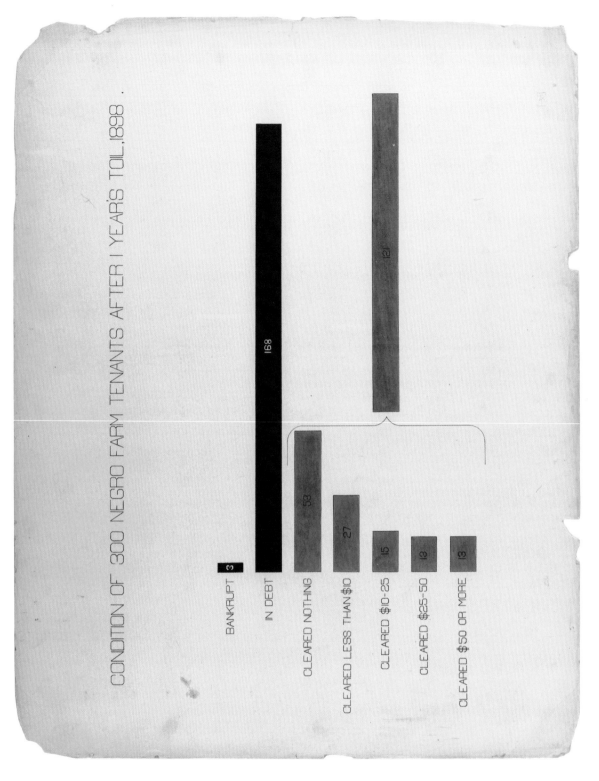

CONDITION OF 300 NEGRO FARM TENANTS AFTER I YEARS TOIL.1898.

BANKRUPT 3

IN DEBT 168

CLEARED NOTHING 53

CLEARED LESS THAN $10 27

CLEARED $10-25 15

CLEARED $25-50 18

CLEARED $50 OR MORE 13

121

Plate 30 Reversing the contemporary use
of black in economics to represent profit and red
to represent loss, this bar chart paints a strong
picture of financial hardship for black farm tenants
at the turn of the century.

Plate 31 Representing 150 black Atlanta families, the layout of this data visualization is strikingly contemporary in its complexity and variety of media. It features a mixed media palette of inked typography, charts colored in gouache, photographic prints, photomechanical reproductions of type, and even gold-leaf painting in a seal in the upper-left corner. Organizing the family budgets into bar charts by class, pastel-colored subcategories are shown for rent, food, clothing, direct taxes, and other expenses. These are linked by fine black lines to a complex grid containing representative images, detailed breakdowns of diets, and poetic descriptions of funds for savings. The use of connecting lines, arrows, and delicate braces creates a spatial feast for the eye. Despite the overwhelming amount of information on display, it is digestible. There is even a note at the bottom of the diagram suggesting that the viewer "raise this frame" to see more information. This is a direct instructional reference to the double-sided, movable standards on "wing frames" that fairgoers could lift and turn, and to the two data sets that follow here (plates 32 and 33).[19]

INCOME AND EXPENDITURE OF 150 NEGRO FAMILIES IN ATLANTA, GA., U.S.A.

ANNUAL EXPENDITURE FOR

RENT. FOOD. CLOTHES. DIRECT TAXES. OTHER EXPENSES AND SAVINGS.

THE STATE TAX RATE IS:
1880—$3.50 PER $1,000
1885—$3.50 "
1890—$3.96 "
1895—$4.56 "
1899—$5.38 "
STATE AND COUNTY TAXES RAISE THIS TO $21 PER $1,000 IN ATLANTA.

THE HIGHER LIFE:
RELIGION.
ART.
EDUCATION.
SICKNESS.
SAVINGS.
AMUSEMENTS.
BOOKS AND PAPERS.
TRAVEL

DIETARY OF WELL-TO-DO NEGRO FAMILY FROM BULLETIN U.S. DEPARTMENT OF AGRICULTURE NO 71.

ANNUAL INCOME

UNITED STATES OF AMERICA — ONE DOLLAR

CLASS	ACTUAL AVERAGE
$ 100-200	$ 139.10
$ 200-300	$249.45
$ 300-400	$335.66
$ 400-500	$433.82
$ 500-750	$547
$ 750-1000	$880
1,000 AND OVER	$1125

POOR
FAIR
COMFORTABLE
WELL-TO-DO

Bar percentages:

- $100-200: 19% · 43% · 28% · 9.9%
- $200-300: 22% · 47% · 23% · 4% · 4%
- $300-400: 23% · 43% · 18% · 4.5% · 11.5%
- $400-500: 18% · 37% · 15% · 5.5% · 24.5%
- $500-750: 13% · 31% · 17% · 5% · 34%
- $750-1000: 37% · 19% · 8% · 36%
- 1,000 AND OVER: 29% · 16% · 4.5% · 50.5%

FOR FURTHER STATISTICS RAISE THIS FRAME.

Plate 32 In this table, budgets of eight black families are arranged in a tight grid containing a complex set of typographic and hand-lettered styles. This is the same data used in the previous plate but rendered in greater numerical detail. It would be viewable after lifting the winged frame of *Income and Expenditure of 150 Negro Families in Atlanta, GA, U.S.A.* Headings are inked in finely engineered capitals listing the occupations of each head of the household and each total family annual income. Notably, the fireman's and engineer's households make the least, and the painter's household earns the most. A list of questions and attributes of the family, from their working hours to their medical bills, is shown in serifed type. Answers to these entries are handwritten with a variety of approaches to penmanship. These hands are likely those of Du Bois's Atlanta researchers, evoking a range of diverse voices.

FAMILY BUDGETS.

FIREMAN AND ENGINEER $312.

SASH AND BLIND MAKER $360.

CARPENTER $360.

ROCK MASON $375.

WHEELWRIGHT $450.

BARBER $400.

BLACKSMITH $450.

PAINTER $540.

Plate 33 This design appears on the reverse side of the previous *Family Budgets* table. The same eight-part grid, body copy style, and hand-written entries are visible behind a layer of brown paper accidentally stuck on the board. The title and headlines are sketched in pencil. This work shows the complexity of translating numeric data into a pencil-drawn layout that would later be lettered or typeset, inked, and finally colored with gouache.

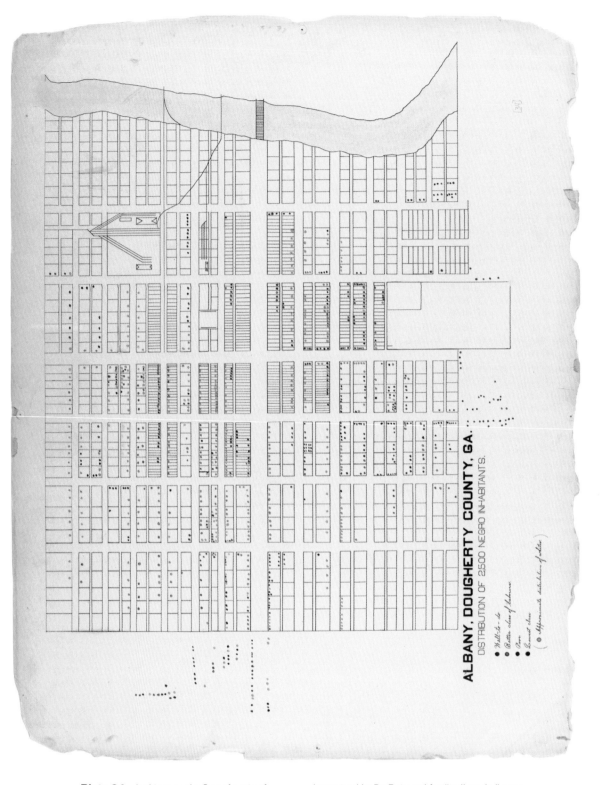

ALBANY, DOUGHERTY COUNTY, GA.

DISTRIBUTION OF 2500 NEGRO INHABITANTS.

● Well-to-do
● Better class of laborers
● Poor
● Lowest class
(● approximate distribution of white)

Plate 34 In this map, the first of a trio of detailed maps of Georgia counties, Du Bois and his team show both visual dexterity and the detailed rigor of the research presented, which includes data of residential areas within the state. The intricate geometry created by the town and city grid is populated with color-coded dots that map the class distribution in black communities in select parts of the state.[20] Four colors represent classes determined by Du Bois: red for "well-to-do," green for "better class of laborers," navy blue for "poor," and black for "lowest class." A final yellow dot is used for the general positioning of white residents. The script-based typography is a departure from the more engineered template lettering used in the keys for most of the other maps, yet another sign of a larger group of makers at work.

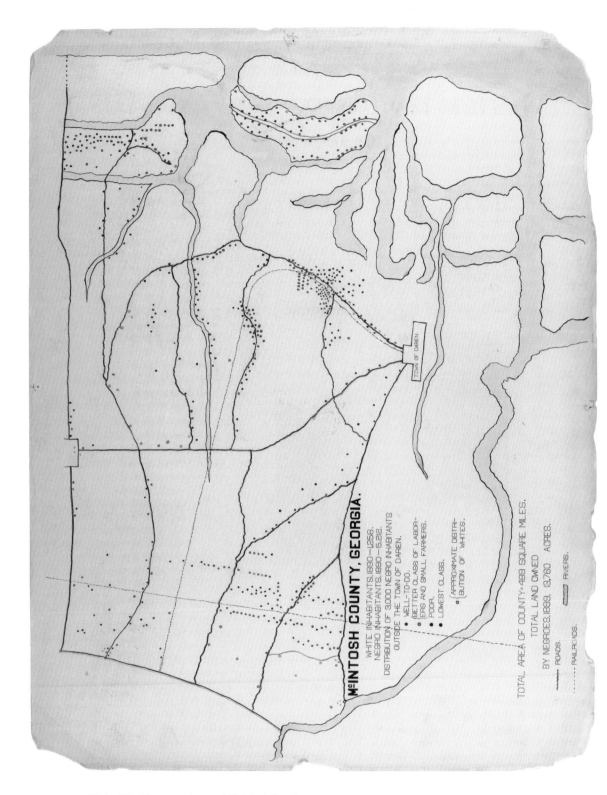

McINTOSH COUNTY, GEORGIA.

WHITE INHABITANTS, 1890 — 1,258.
NEGRO INHABITANTS, 1890 — 5,212.
DISTRIBUTION OF 3,000 NEGRO INHABITANTS
OUTSIDE THE TOWN OF DARIEN.

• WELL-TO-DO.
• BETTER CLASS OF LABORERS AND SMALL FARMERS.
• POOR.
• LOWEST CLASS.
• (APPROXIMATE DISTRIBUTION OF WHITES.

TOTAL AREA OF COUNTY·499 SQUARE MILES.
TOTAL LAND OWNED
BY NEGROES, 1899, 13,760 ACRES.

──── ROADS.
‒‒‒‒ RAILROADS.
──── RIVERS.

TOWN OF DARIEN.

Plate 35   The second map, of McIntosh County,
zooms out to a wider perspective showing roads,
railways, and rivers in the rural areas surrounding
the town of Darien, Georgia. A key of dots continues
the system of black class distribution across the
county. The pair of keys, one for the population
distribution and the other for the geographic aspects,
uses slight size variations in engineered lettering.

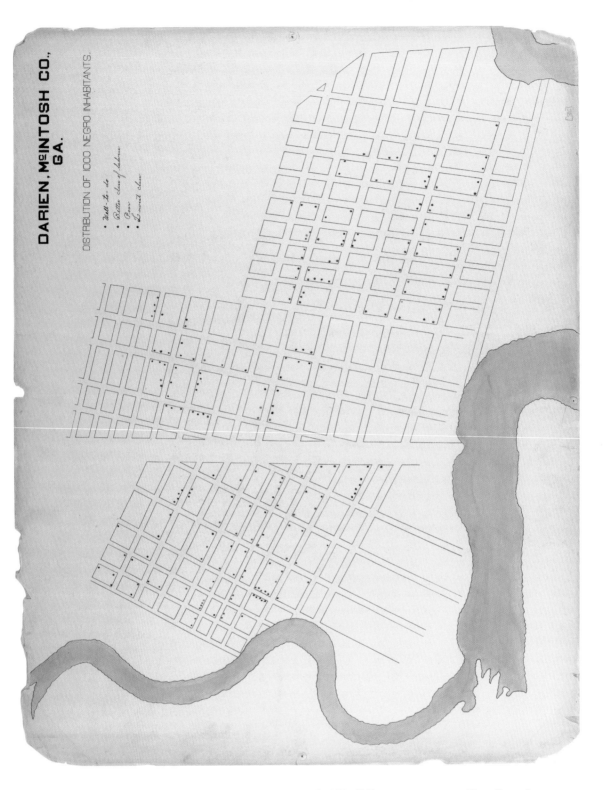

Plate 36 The final map in the trio is an expand-ed detail of the previous map focusing on the town of Darien, Georgia. An idyllic costal town, Darien might have been chosen by Du Bois because of its ties to the shipping and lumber industries that employed many black workers, or because of a notorious looting by Union soldiers during the Civil War.[21] The town is represented by a diagonal grid of streets bordered in the west and south by a curving river. Although the key uses the same colors as the previous two county maps, small variations in language and typeface suggest a collective of designers working at great speed.

Part II
A Series of Statistical Charts Illustrating
the Condition of the Descendants of
Former African Slaves Now Resident in
the United States of America

All boards are approximately 22 × 28 inches, rendered in ink and watercolor.[22]

Plate 37 Designed as a proclamation in type and image form, the first panel in the second series is among the most dense. It is also the most self-referential, describing the subject of black Americans in Georgia while also pointing to Atlanta University as a collective author of the data visualizations to follow. The palette of gouache in bright colors continues from the Georgia study. All the charts that follow feature a strategic mix of typographical families and styles. The principal type appears to be a sans serif or grotesque typeface, which predates the twentieth century. Closer inspection reveals that the predominant letter style used in the charts has no curves—only straight lines—and is more akin to lettering generated by templates designed for architectural or engineering plans. Based on the authors' training in sociology rather than graphic design, it would make sense for the Atlanta University students to have used some templates and pre-existing tools. The residue of technical lettering, most likely from an American architectural letter template, is especially visible in the lighter weights of the hand-rendered type utilized for the French translations, evidenced by the non-standard weight of heavier diacritical marks (accents).

A SERIES OF STATISTICAL CHARTS, ILLUSTRA- TING THE CONDITION OF THE DESCENDANTS OF FOR- MER AFRICAN SLAVES NOW RESIDENT IN THE UNITED STATES OF AMERICA.

UNE SÉRIE DE CARTES ET DIAGRAMMES STATISTIQUES MONTRANT LA CONDITION PRÉSENTE DES DESCENDANTS DES ANCIENS ESCLAVES AFRI- CAINS ACTUELLMENT ÉTABLIS DANS LES ETATS UNIS D'AMÉRIQUE.

PREPARED AND EXECUTED BY
NEGRO STUDENTS UNDER THE
DIRECTION OF
ATLANTA UNIVERSITY,
ATLANTA, GA.,
UNITED STATES OF AMERICA.

PRÉPARÉES ET EXÉCUTÉES PAR
DES ÉTUDIANTS NÈGRES SOUS
LA DIRECTION DE L' UNIVERSITÉ
D'ATLANTA,
ÉTAT DE GÉORGIE.
ETATS UNIS D'AMERIQUE.

■ ★ CENTRE OF NEGRO POPULATION.
ATLANTA UNIVERSITY.

THE UNIVERSITY WAS FOUNDED IN 1867. IT HAS INSTRUCTED 6000 NEGRO STUDENTS.
L' UNIVERSITÉ A ÉTÉ FONDÉE EN 1867. ELLE A DONNÉ L'INSTRUCTION A 6000 ÉTUDIANTS NEGRES.
IT HAS GRADUATED 330 NEGROES AMONG WHOM ARE:
ELLE A DÉLIVRE DES DIPLOMES A 330 NEGRES DONT :

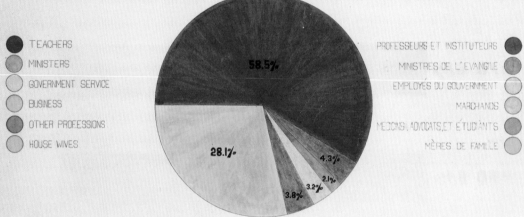

● TEACHERS
○ MINISTERS
○ GOVERNMENT SERVICE
○ BUSINESS
○ OTHER PROFESSIONS
○ HOUSE WIVES

PROFESSEURS ET INSTITUTEURS ●
MINISTRES DE L'EVANGILE ○
EMPLOYES DU GOUVERMENT ○
MARCHANDS ○
MEDICINS, ADVOCATS, ET ÉTUDIANTS ○
MÈRES DE FAMILLE ○

58,5%
28,1%
4,3%
2,1%
3,2%
3,8%

THE UNIVERSITY HAS 20 PROFESSORS AND INSTRUCTORS AND 250 STUDENTS AT PRESENT.
IT HAS FIVE BUILDINGS, 60 ACRES OF CAMPUS, AND A LIBRARY OF 11,000 VOLUMES. IT AIMS TO RAISE AND CIVILIZE THE SONS OF THE FREEDMEN BY TRAINING THEIR MORE CAPABLE MEMBERS IN THE LIBER- AL ARTS ACCORDING TO THE BEST STANDARDS OF THE DAY.
THE PROPER ACCOMPLISHMENT OF THIS WORK DEMANDS AN ENDOWMENT FUND OF $500,000.

L' UNIVERSITÉ A ACTUELLEMENT 20 PROFESSEURS ET INSTRUCTEURS ET 250 ÉTUDIANTS.
ELLE EST COMPOSÉE DE CINC BÂTIMENTS, 60 ACRES (ENVIRON 26 HECTARES) DE TERRAIN SERVANT DE COUR ET DE CHAMP DE RÉCRÉATION, ET D'UNE BIBLIOTHÉQUE CONTENANT 11,000 VOLUMES.
SON BUT EST D'ÉLEVER ET DE CIVILISER LES FILS DES NÈGRES AFFRANCHIS EN DONNANT AUX MIEUX DOUÉS UNE ÉDUCATION DANS LES ARTS LIBÉRAUX EN ACCORD AVEC LES IDÉES LES PLUS PROGRES – SISTES DE L'ÉPOQUE.
L' ACCOMPLISSEMENT DE CETTE ŒUVRE DEMANDE UNE DOTATION DE $500,000 (2,500,000 FRANCS).

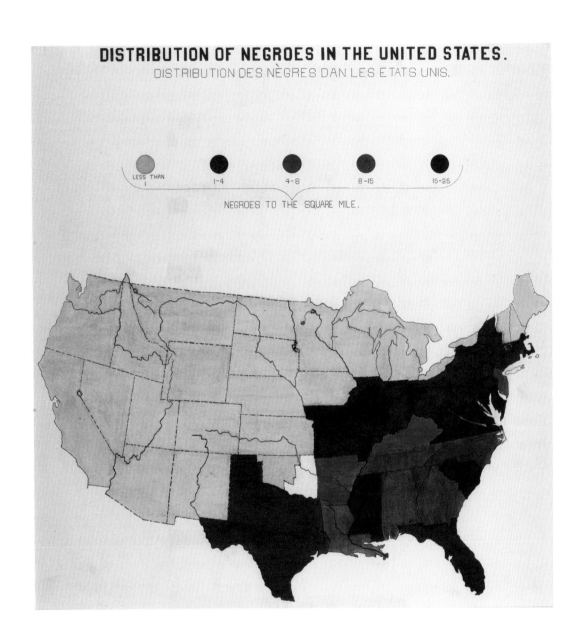

DISTRIBUTION OF NEGROES IN THE UNITED STATES.

DISTRIBUTION DES NÈGRES DAN LES ETATS UNIS.

LESS THAN 1   1-4   4-8   8-15   15-25

NEGROES TO THE SQUARE MILE.

Plate 38 This map of the United States represents the overall distribution of black Americans in 1890. A key of circles filled with colors favored by Du Bois and his team appear above the nation, with yellow, blue, red, brown, and black corresponding to increasing density. It is common across all of the charts that darker and more saturated colors are usually used for statistics with greater value, density, or importance. The technique here connects to similar heat map strategies used elsewhere.

Increase of the Negro population in the United States of America.

Accroissement de la population Negre aux Etats Unis d' Amerique.

Done by Atlanta University.

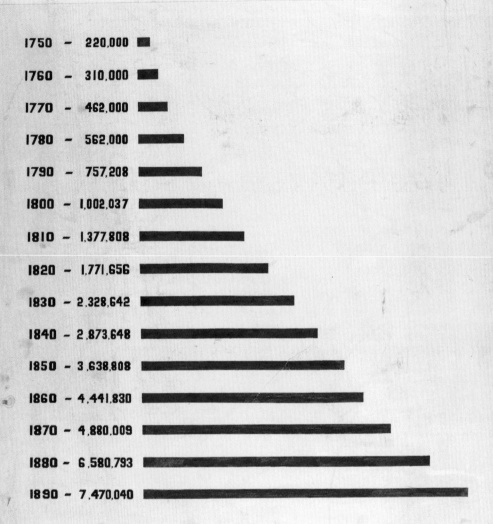

1750 – 220,000	■
1760 – 310,000	■
1770 – 462,000	■
1780 – 562,000	■
1790 – 757,208	■
1800 – 1,002,037	■
1810 – 1,377,808	■
1820 – 1,771,656	■
1830 – 2,328,642	■
1840 – 2,873,648	■
1850 – 3,638,808	■
1860 – 4,441,830	■
1870 – 4,880,009	■
1880 – 6,580,793	■
1890 – 7,470,040	■

Plate 39 Population is a common subject
of many of the charts generated by the Atlanta
University team. The data set depicted here
is unique in that it covers a span of 140 years.
This chart also deploys both old-style typography
and engineered templated lettering.

Plate 40 Charting data back to the late eighteenth century, this line chart compares populations of blacks and whites by total number instead of by the rate of growth, as depicted in the previous chart. Key socioeconomic events are mapped on the grid, this time with a mix of domestic and international forces. The abolition of the slave trade, immigration from Europe, and Emancipation are noted as key influences on both populations. The inclusion of "the suppression of slave trade" on the chart also resonates with the title and topic of Du Bois's 1896 dissertation, *The Suppression of the African Slave-Trade to the United States of America.*[23] Visually, this chart's lettering style and craft in regards to rendering varies considerably from the previous two line charts (plates 7 and 21). Key differences include the use of small capitals in the engineered lettering for the word *millions*, and a uniquely ornate hand-lettered style for the key.

Comparative rate of increase of the White and Negro elements of the population of the United States.

Accroissement proportionnel des elements blancs et noirs aux Etats Unis.

Done by Atlanta University.

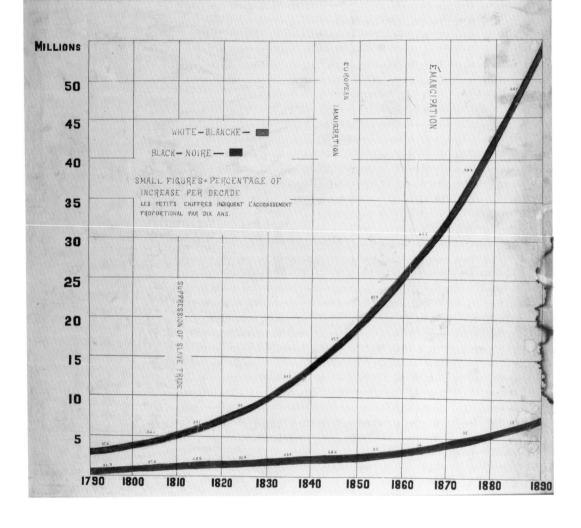

MILLIONS

WHITE — BLANCHE —

BLACK — NOIRE —

SMALL FIGURES = PERCENTAGE OF
INCREASE PER DECADE
LES PETITS CHIFFRES INDIQUENT L'ACCROISSEMENT
PROPORTIONAL PAR DIX ANS.

EUROPEAN IMMIGRATION

EMANCIPATION

SUPPRESSION OF SLAVE TRADE

1790 1800 1810 1820 1830 1840 1850 1860 1870 1880 1890

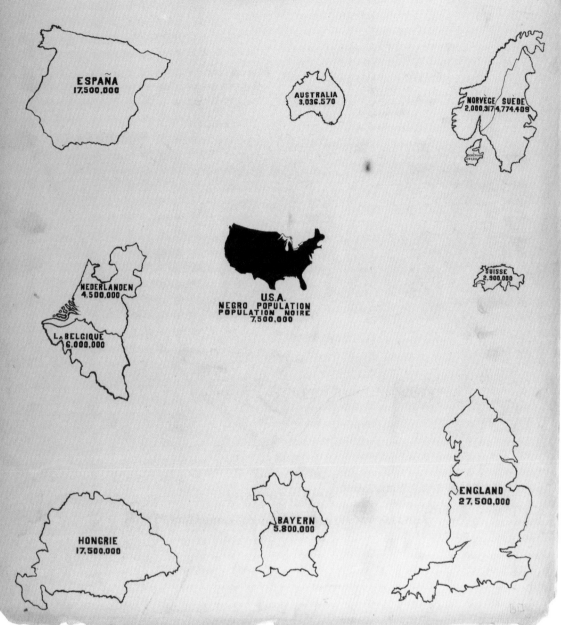

NEGRO POPULATION OF THE UNITED STATES COMPARED WITH THE TOTAL POPULATION OF OTHER COUNTRIES .

POPULATION NÈGRE DES ETATS UNIS COMPARÉE À LA POPULATION TOTALE DES AUTRES PAYS .

DONE BY ATLANTA UNIVERSITY .

ESPAÑA
17,500,000

AUSTRALIA
3,036,570

NORVÈGE SUEDE
2,000,317 4,774,409

NEDERLANDEN
4,500,000

L. BELGIQUE
6,000,000

U.S.A.
NEGRO POPULATION
POPULATION NOIRE
7,500,000

SUISSE
2,900,000

HONGRIE
17,500,000

BAYERN
5,800,000

ENGLAND
27,500,000

Plate 41   In this diagram, a solid black United States with a red outline is centered around strategically chosen European nations, all drawn from the perspective of the Mercator projection.[24] The European nations are scaled to a relative size for quick visual comparison of total population.

The typography of the headline and the country labels is more condensed than the typography in the Georgia study. This typographic variance between the two series supports the idea that different teams of makers were dispatched by Du Bois to ensure production in time for the Paris Exposition.

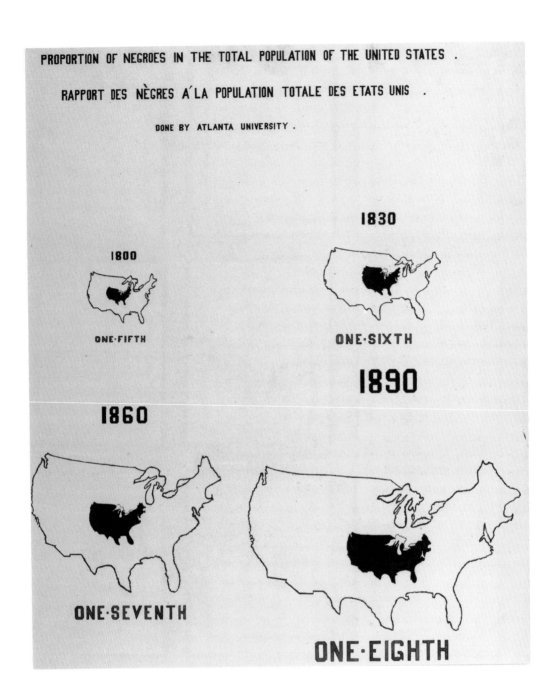

PROPORTION OF NEGROES IN THE TOTAL POPULATION OF THE UNITED STATES .

RAPPORT DES NÈGRES A'LA POPULATION TOTALE DES ETATS UNIS .

DONE BY ATLANTA UNIVERSITY .

1800
ONE·FIFTH

1830
ONE·SIXTH

1890

1860
ONE·SEVENTH

ONE·EIGHTH

Plate 42 This companion to the previous map also uses geographic scale as a key comparative tool. The black population of the United States is shown to be growing over the nineteenth century with a scale shift in the country outlines. The type size of the year and proportional labels changes according to the size of the country. The color palette of red, green, and black is a likely allusion to the Pan-African flag. Red symbolizes blood shed for freedom, black the hue of the skin of people of African descent, and green the lush landscape of the motherland.[25] Du Bois's connections with Pan-African movements in the United States and abroad are a natural source for the tricolor config-uration that recurs in a number of the plates.[26]

Plate 43   Three towering bars stack information on the occupations of black Georgians according to the worker's gender. This diagram translates both the heading and the key into the French text that cascades vertically down each bar. The varying sizes, alignments, and positions of the typography continue to imply the work of multiple hands.

Occupations in which American Negroes are engaged.

Occupations et industries des Nègres Americains.

Done by Atlanta University.

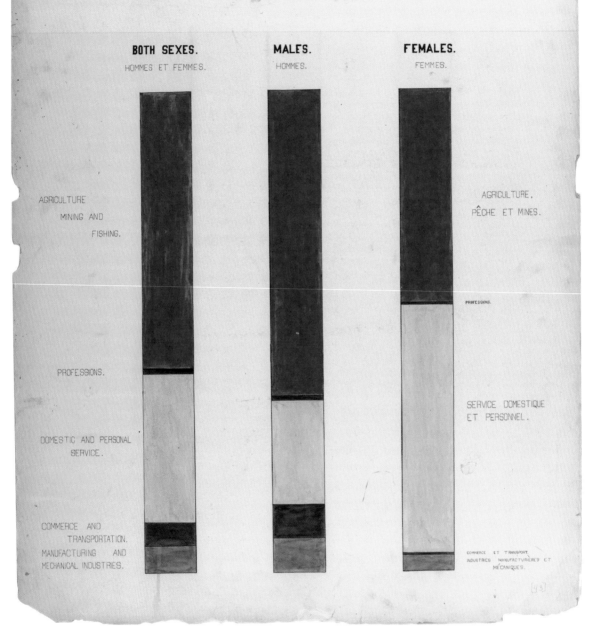

BOTH SEXES.
HOMMES ET FEMMES.

MALES.
HOMMES.

FEMALES.
FEMMES.

AGRICULTURE
MINING AND
FISHING.

AGRICULTURE.
PÊCHE ET MINES.

PROFESSIONS.

PROFESSIONS.

DOMESTIC AND PERSONAL
SERVICE.

SERVICE DOMESTIQUE
ET PERSONNEL.

COMMERCE AND
TRANSPORTATION.
MANUFACTURING AND
MECHANICAL INDUSTRIES.

COMMERCE ET TRANSPORT.
INDUSTRIES MANUFACTURIERES ET
MÉCANIQUES.

Plate 44   Outlined in a deep red, five graphic
black slices of ink representing black workers
in a range of professions confront the viewer in a
pinwheel design. At first glance the circle chart
structure is obscured by the intense contrast
between these dark shapes and their white-hatched
counterparts, which represent white workers.
Further inspection shows meticulous detail in a red
circle inscribed with categories contained by tabs
that are met with tiny arrows drawn in graphite.
The English and French headings and a credit to
Atlanta University are typeset in an alternative
serif that is used in the headings for a third of the
plates. The origin of this old-style typeface can
be traced to late fifteenth-century European
printing, especially in Italy.[27] The regularity of
the type size, consistency of individual forms, and
pencil-drawn hang line for type placement suggest
these headings were generated by letterpress or
offset printing.[28] The details in this chart indicate
that the diagrams were likely first composed in
pencil and then finished with ink and gouache.

Proportion of Whites and Negroes in the different classes of occupation in the United States.

Proportion des blancs et des Nègres dans les diverses especes d' occupations en Amerique.

Done by Atlanta University.

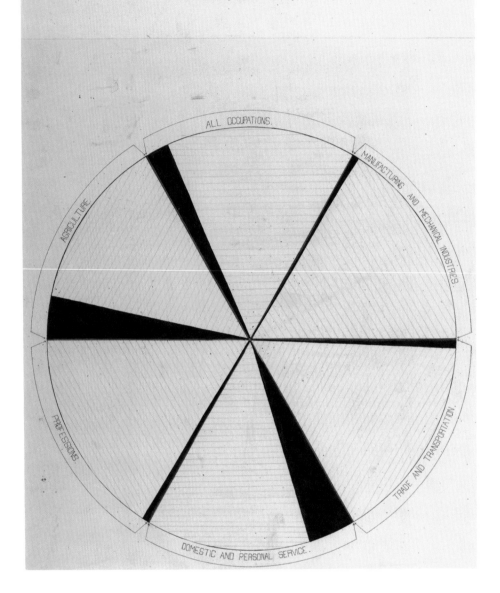

ALL OCCUPATIONS.

MANUFACTURING AND MECHANICAL INDUSTRIES.

AGRICULTURE

TRADE AND TRANSPORTATION.

PROFESSIONS

DOMESTIC AND PERSONAL SERVICE.

Occupations in which 10,000 or more American Negroes are engaged.

Emplois occupant au moins 10,000 Nègres Americains.

Done by Atlanta University.

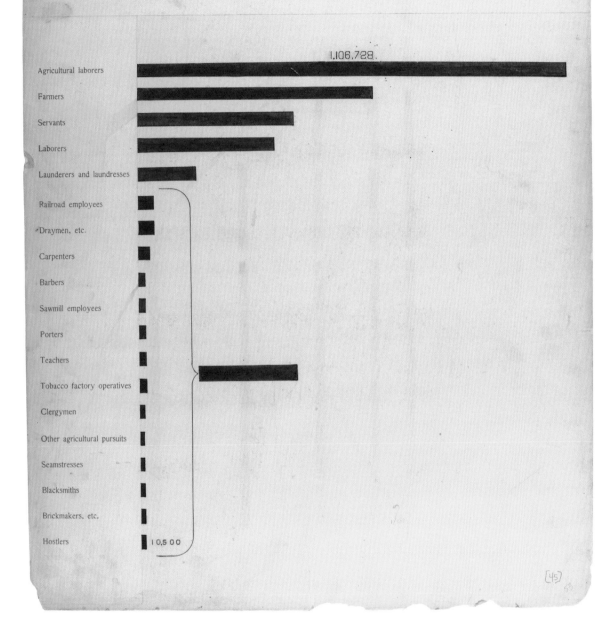

1,106,728.

- Agricultural laborers
- Farmers
- Servants
- Laborers
- Launderers and laundresses
- Railroad employees
- Draymen, etc.
- Carpenters
- Barbers
- Sawmill employees
- Porters
- Teachers
- Tobacco factory operatives
- Clergymen
- Other agricultural pursuits
- Seamstresses
- Blacksmiths
- Brickmakers, etc.
- Hostlers

10,500

Plate 45 Built around a list of professions, this bar chart depicts in strong contrast the imbalance in roles for black workers. A long, bright red bar representing agricultural labor dominates a descending stream of farmers, servants, and other laborers. A final group with very detailed job titles includes barbers, sawmill operators, tobacco factory workers, and seamstresses. This small, widely varied group presents a "long tail" of more skilled occupations.[29]

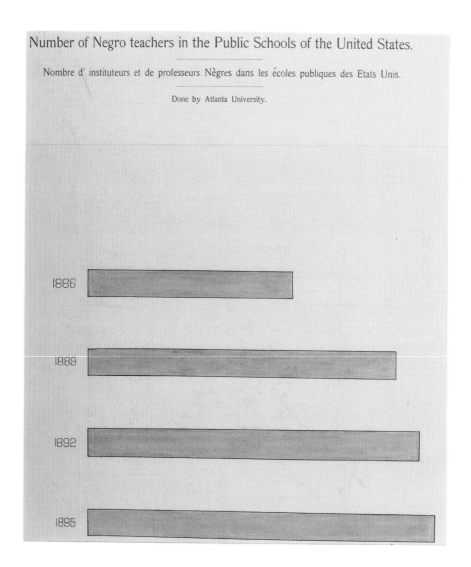

Number of Negro teachers in the Public Schools of the United States.

Nombre d' instituteurs et de professeurs Nègres dans les écoles publiques des Etats Unis.

Done by Atlanta University.

1886

1889

1892

1895

Plate 46 Here, Du Bois is strategic in his use of statistical detail. Highlighting the noble profession of the schoolteacher, this bright yellow bar chart covers only nine years. However, by foregrounding this small data set, Du Bois emphasizes that education, along with population growth and property ownership, is critical to black self-determination.

P 1124

Illiteracy of the American Negroes compared with that of other nations.

Proportion d' illettrés parmi les Nègres Americains comparée à celle des autres nations.

Done by Atlanta University.

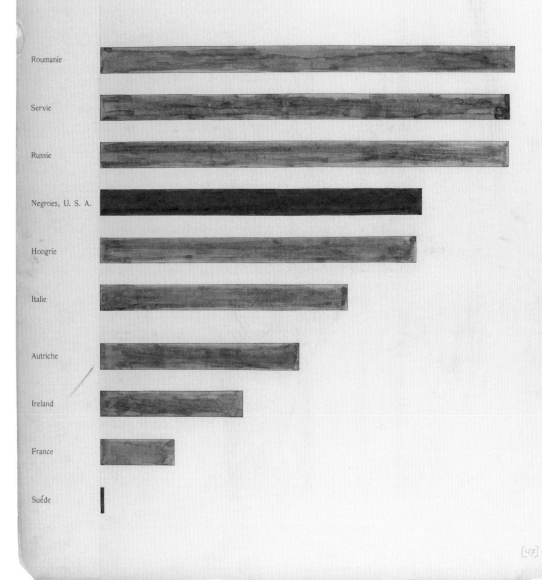

Roumanie

Servie

Russie

Negroes, U. S. A.

Hongrie

Italie

Autriche

Ireland

France

Suéde

[47]

Plate 47 A bright red bar set in a horizontal grouping of green bars compares the illiteracy of black Americans to other nations participating in the Paris Exposition. In order to correct misconceptions about the education of black Americans, Du Bois compares the United States to other countries with rates of greater and lesser illiteracy. The key is written in French only, an indicator that Du Bois and his team sought to target the fair's European audience.

Enrollment in the Negro common schools of the former slave States of the United States.

Inscriptions dans les écoles primaires des anciens états esclaves des Etats Unis.

Done by Atlanta University.

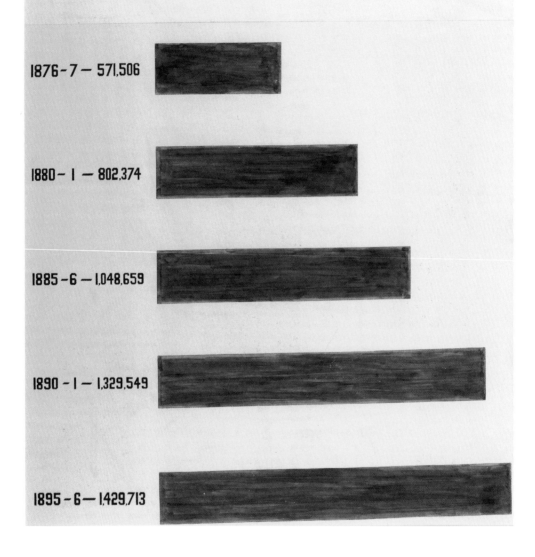

1876-7 — 571,506

1880-1 — 802,374

1885-6 — 1,048,659

1890-1 — 1,329,549

1895-6 — 1,429,713

Plate 48   Based in part on his own life experience, Du Bois knew that education was a critical indicator of social and economic equality. This brown chart clearly references skin tone and boldly demonstrates educational progress for states that would later regress with the impact of Jim Crow laws.[30]

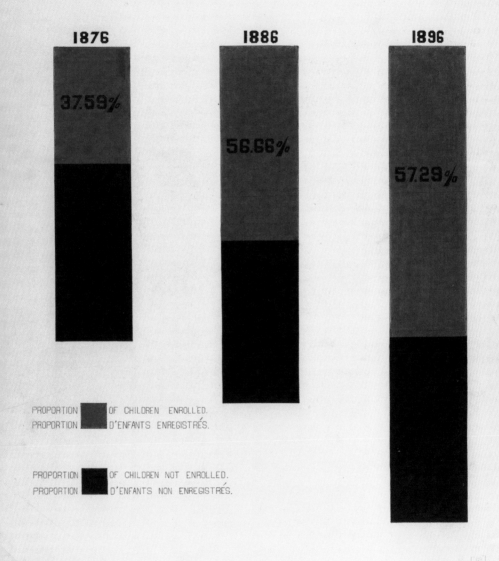

PROPORTION OF TOTAL NEGRO CHILDREN OF SCHOOL AGE WHO ARE ENROLLED IN THE PUBLIC SCHOOLS.

PROPORTION DES ENFANTS NÈGRES EN ÂGE D'ÉCOLE ENREGISTRÉS DANS LES ÉCOLES PUBLIQUES.

DONE BY ATLANTA UNIVERSITY.

1876

37.59%

1886

56.66%

1896

57.29%

PROPORTION ▭ OF CHILDREN ENROLLED.
PROPORTION ▭ D'ENFANTS ENREGISTRÉS.

PROPORTION ▮ OF CHILDREN NOT ENROLLED.
PROPORTION ▮ D'ENFANTS NON ENREGISTRÉS.

Plate 49 In this bar chart, the shapes, figures, and typography grow bolder and more graphic. Black and red rectangles are combined with bold numbers that show a steady increase in the enrollment of school-age children of color after Emancipation.

THE RISE OF THE NEGROES FROM SLAVERY TO FREEDOM IN ONE GENERATION.

PROGRÈS GRADUEL DES NÈGRES DE L'ESCLAVAGE À LA LIBERTÉ EN UNE GÉNÉRATION.

DONE BY ATLANTA UNIVERSITY.

1890

IN 1890 NEARLY ONE FIFTH OF THEM OWNED THEIR OWN HOMES AND FARMS.
THIS ADVANCE WAS ACCOMPLISHED ENTIRELY WITHOUT STATE AID, AND IN THE
FACE OF PROSCRIPTIVE LAWS.

EN 1890 ENVIRON UN CINQUIÈME ÉTAIENT PROPRIÉTAIRES DE LEURS HAB-
ITATIONS ET DE LEURS FERMES. CE PROGRÈS S'EST ACCOMPLI SANS
SECOURS AUCUN DE L'ETAT ET EN PRÉSENCE DE LOIS DÉFAVORABLES.

19%
PEASANT PROPRIETORS
PAYSANS PROPRIÉTAIRES

IN 1860 NEARLY 90% OF THE BLACKS WERE SLAVES.

EN 1860 ENVIRON 90% DES NÈGRES ÉTAIENT ESCLAVES.

81%
TENANTS
MÉTAYERS

1860

11%
FREE LABORERS
OUVRIERS LIBRES

89%
SLAVES
ESCLAVES

Plate 50 Both a proclamation and a diagram, this display of the rapid transformation from slave laborers to a mix of tenants and landholders is mapped across a pair of saturated bars. Again using the Pan-African colors of red, black, and green, the bars read like hanging protest banners. Fine dotted lines of ink appear like an explosion on the page, showing the increase in free laborers from 11 percent in 1860 to 81 percent in 1890. The narrative of black self-determination is further emphasized here with a note that black home and land ownership "was accomplished entirely without state aid and in the face of proscriptive laws."

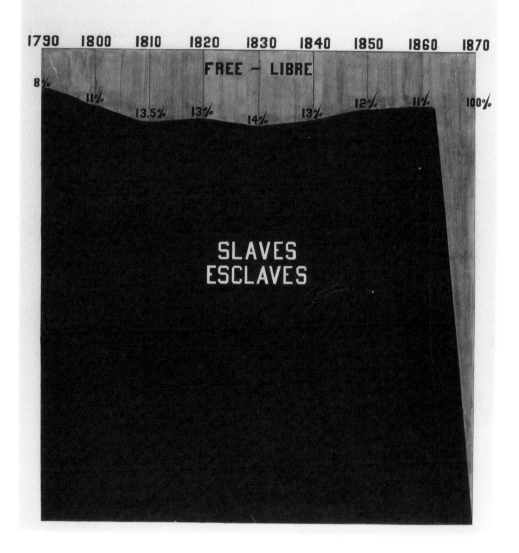

PROPORTION OF FREEMEN AND SLAVES AMONG AMERICAN NEGROES .

PROPORTION DES NÈGRES LIBRES ET DES ESCLAVES EN AMÉRIQUE .

DONE BY ATLANTA UNIVERSITY .

1790　1800　1810　1820　1830　1840　1850　1860　1870

FREE — LIBRE

8%

11%

13.5%　13%

14%

13%

12%

11%

100%

SLAVES
ESCLAVES

Plate 51 This area chart uses similar information as *Slaves and Free Negroes* (plate 12) but renders it on a national level and in a completely different way. The chronology reads left to right, and green and black are used instead of red. The Atlanta group may have been motivated to make different but related visual interpretations by a desire to explore how varied forms might be read by the audience in new ways.

CITY AND RURAL POPULATION AMONG AMERICAN NEGROES IN THE FORMER SLAVE STATES .

POPULATION DES NÈGRES HABITANT LES VILLES ET DE CEUX HABITANT LES COMPAGNES DANS LES ANCIENS

ETATS ESCLAVES .   DONE BY ATLANTA UNIVERSITY.

PROPORTION [   ] LIVING IN CITIES OF 8,000 INHABITANTS OR MORE.
PROPORTION DANS LES VILLES DE 8,000 HABITANTS OU PLUS.

PROPORTION [   ] LIVING IN VILLAGES AND COUNTRY DISTRICTS
PROPORTION DANS LES VILLAGES ET LES COMPAGNES

1860 4.2%   **95.8%**

1870 8.5%   **91.5%**

1880 8.4%   **91.6%**

1890 12%   **88%**

Plate 52 Four black and red bars represent
the number of African Americans dwelling in urban
and rural areas. The red portion of each bar sig-
nifies the urban populations and the disproportion-
ately long swaths of black show how much rural
residency has dominated the black experience in
Georgia, both before and after Emancipation.

Plate 53 This complex grid, area chart, and bar chart is a vibrating combination of color and shape. Split down the middle into "males" and "females," each half of the nearly symmetrical chart is further broken down by color-coded grids: a green zone for widows and widowers, a red zone for married couples, and a blue zone for single people—the data set is closely related to plate 10. The typography is laid out with a tight structure around the outside of the colored matrix. However, inside the grid, type is set at dynamic angles in a manner that would later become a hallmark of 1920s Russian constructivism and the 1960s conceptual text-based art of Lawrence Weiner.[31] Here, similar to Weiner's body of work, a distinct rigid typographic treatment is used as an image to reinforce a repeated conceptual motif.

Conjugal condition of American Negroes according to age periods.

Condition conjugale des Nègres Americains au point de vue de l' age.

Done by Atlanta University.

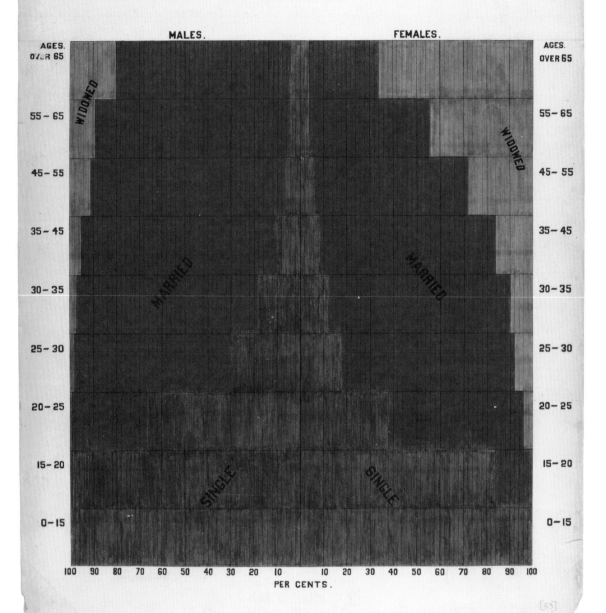

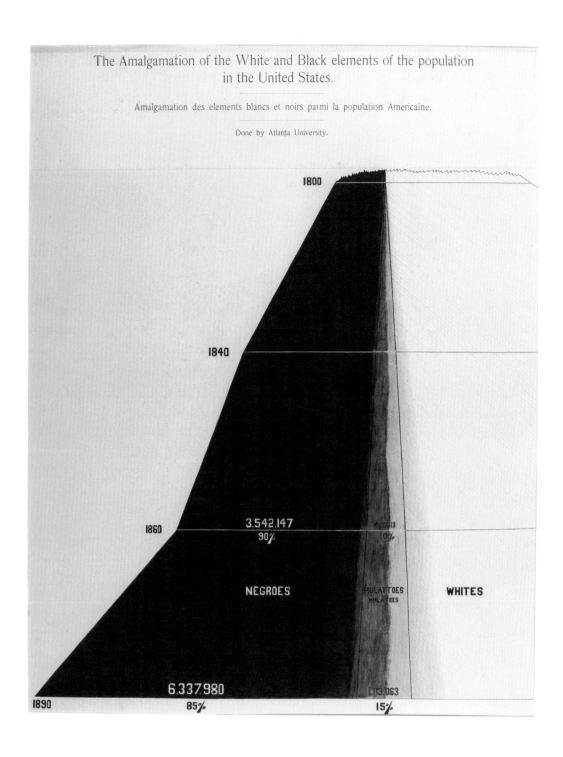

The Amalgamation of the White and Black elements of the population
in the United States.

Amalgamation des elements blancs et noirs parmi la population Americaine.

Done by Atlanta University.

1800

1840

1860   3.542.147
        90%   10%

NEGROES   MULATTOES   WHITES
                 MULÂTRES

        6.337.980   1.113.063
1890   85%   15%

Plate 54   This data portrait of race in the United
States comes in the form of a gradient-colored area
chart shaped like a mountain peak. Here, a spectrum
of "blacks," "mulattoes," and "whites" are mapped
over a century. Shades of blacks, browns, yellows,
cross-hatching, and the white of the page articulate
a racial binary as well as more fluid identities.

Proprietes contribuables des Nègres dans trois Etats des Etats Unis.

Done by Atlanta University.

VIRGINIA.
1895
$ 13,933,998

NORTH CAROLINA.
1891
$ 8,018,446

GEORGIA.
1895
$ 12,941,230

TOTAL
$ 34,893,684
OR
180,796,290 FRANCS.

Plate 55 While not apparent at first glance, the dollar amounts of black-owned property in three states rendered here are not proportionally scaled. This is especially true of the bottom figure, which represents the total of all three. The four triangles in red, brown, blue, and black with type become an insignia of black-owned land, rather than a true visual interpretation of the property values in three Southern states. The end result would feel at home as part of a nautical semaphore flag set or in a mid-twentieth-century modernist painting exhibition.

Plate 56   This plate uses black and white bars to represent the proportion of black landowners to renters in nine Southern states. Minimal and spare, the use of flat black gouache for the tenants focuses the eye and mind on the significance of the large masses of black Southerners who did not own their own land.

Negro landholders in various States of the United States.

Proprietaires fonciers Nègres dans plusieurs Etats.

Done by Atlanta University.

OWNERS.   TENANTS.

State	Owners	
Virginia	27%	
South Carolina	18%	
Texas	22%	
North Carolina	19%	
Georgia	12%	
Mississippi	13%	
Tennessee	20%	
Louisiana	12%	
Arkansas	21%	

Plate 57 A jumble of squares defies viewer expectations in a chart depicting the relative number of black men in a range of occupations. Though not arranged alphabetically or by descending density, the unusual spatial configuration uses surface area and dynamic color to reflect imbalances in the representation of men in various fields.

Negro business men in the United States.

Nègres Americains dans les affaires.

Done by Atlanta University.

Estimated capital
Capital évalué

$ 8,784,637
45,516,254 FRANCS.

General merchandise stores
Magazins de provisions et
d' objects divers

Grocers
Epiciers

Bankers
Banquiers

Undertakers
Entrepreneurs de pompes
funebres

Building contractors
Entrepreneurs de batiments

Druggists
Pharmaciens

Publishers
Editeurs

Building and loan associations
Institutions financieres co-oper-
atives

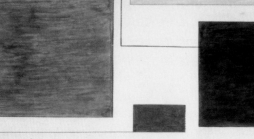

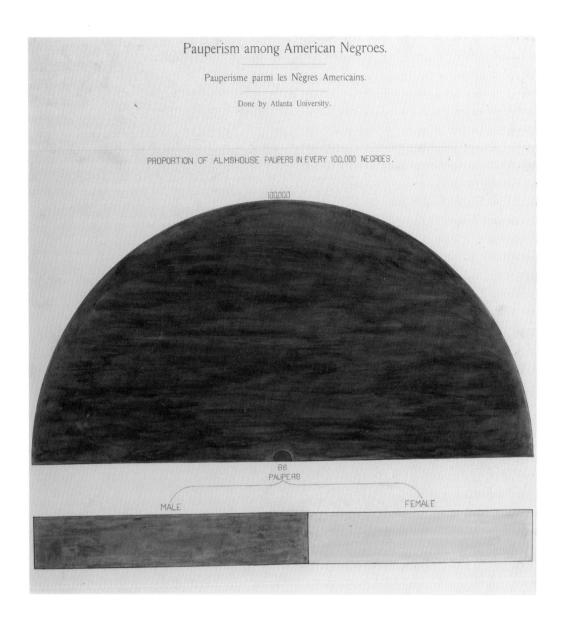

Pauperism among American Negroes.

Pauperisme parmi les Nègres Americains.

Done by Atlanta University.

PROPORTION OF ALMSHOUSE PAUPERS IN EVERY 100,000 NEGROES.

100,000

86
PAUPERS

MALE

FEMALE

Plate 58 This diagram merges a circle chart with a bar graph to express the number and gender of the poorest African Americans in Georgia. A giant brown semicircle stands in for one hundred thousand black people. A tiny bright red semicircle stands in for 86 black paupers within that larger group. The small number of African Americans residing in almshouses reinforces the narrative of black progress and self-reliance that underscores the entire American Negro Exhibit, while hinting at the dearth of national and state aid offered to black people in the nation (see plate 50).

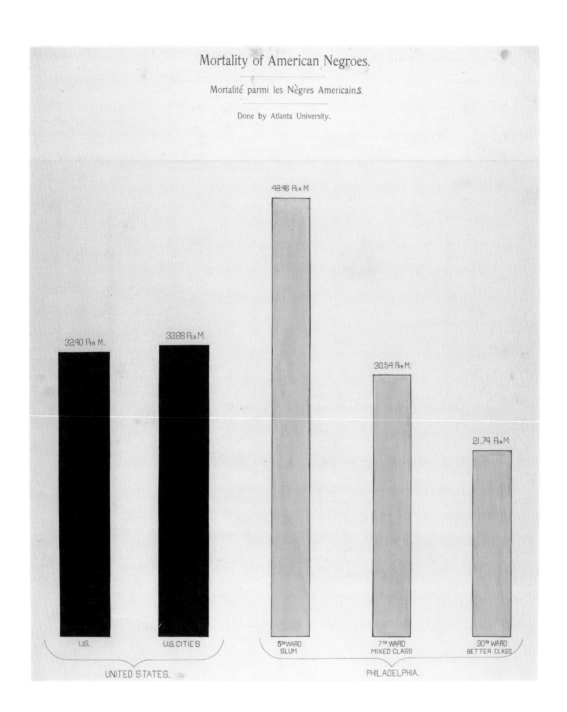

Mortality of American Negroes.

Mortalité parmi les Nègres Americains.

Done by Atlanta University.

Plate 59   Here the mortality rates of black people across the United States and in US cities are quantified as black bars. In comparison, mortality rates in three different neighborhoods of Philadelphia are displayed as bright yellow bars. Du Bois provides a class analysis of the three neighborhoods, showing higher mortality in "slums" and "mixed class" areas than in the "better class" wards. Though these charts were made by the Atlanta University group, the data source is Du Bois's earlier study, *The Philadelphia Negro* (1899).

Crime among American Negroes.

Criminalité parmi les Nègres Americains.

Done by Atlanta University.

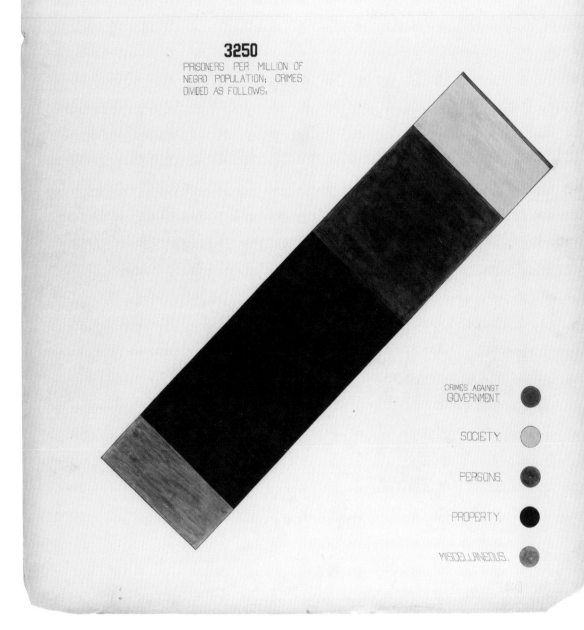

3250

PRISONERS PER MILLION OF
NEGRO POPULATION; CRIMES
DIVIDED AS FOLLOWS:

CRIMES AGAINST
GOVERNMENT.

SOCIETY.

PERSONS.

PROPERTY.

MISCELLANEOUS.

Plate 60   Slanted at a forty-five-degree angle, this chart examines the crimes of 3,250 African Americans. Using a color-labeled ratio of rectangles, the design's dynamic orientation on the page defies the typical bar chart. Its squat width also veers into the genre of an area chart. The bulk of the convictions shown are crimes against people and property that are coded in brown and black, respectively. Societal and miscellaneous crimes follow in yellow and green tones, and a red sliver of governmental crimes tops the graph. The heading, narrative text, and key follow similar compositional principles of other charts, but the word "miscellaneous" is set in a curious contra-italic or backslant italic that is used sporadically in the infographics for visual emphasis.[32]

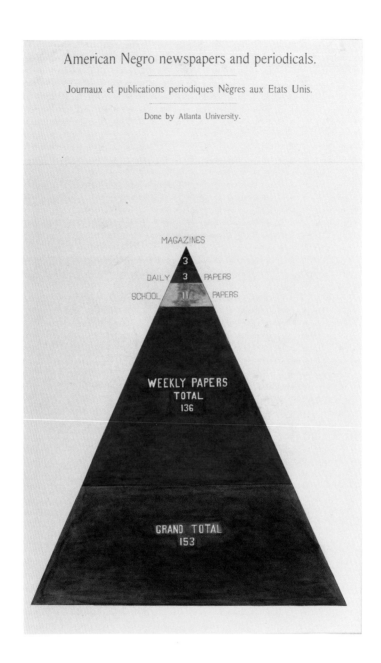

American Negro newspapers and periodicals.

Journaux et publications periodiques Nègres aux Etats Unis.

Done by Atlanta University.

MAGAZINES

3

DAILY 3 PAPERS

SCHOOL 11 PAPERS

WEEKLY PAPERS
TOTAL
136

GRAND TOTAL
153

Plate 61 A hyper-color pyramid presents the numbers and types of African American periodicals in their myriad formats. This totemic structure is designed with efficiency in mind. The 153 news-papers and magazines represented show a rich network of publishing for black audiences. One of these periodicals would bring the American Negro Exhibit full circle: the cover of the November 1900 issue of the *Colored American* shows Thomas J. Calloway, the exhibit organizer and editor of the *Colored American*, sitting in the space of the American Negro Exhibit.

Religion of American Negroes.

Religion des Nègres Americains.

Done by Atlanta University.

Catholics   14,517.

Protestants

Protestant Sects:

Baptists

Methodists

Presbyterians

Congregationalists

Miscellaneous

2.659.460.

Plate 62   This two-part graph examining the religious affiliations of African Americans represents two of the largest branches of Christianity in red and green bars. The Protestant population is further broken down into subsets measured in a series of yellow bars. In the group surveyed, Protestants far outnumber the Catholics, so Du Bois and his team employ one of his trademark "spiral bars" to display and contain the varying data. The bars counting the subsets are lighter and thinner than the major groups, allowing the viewer to digest both aspects of the research over time.

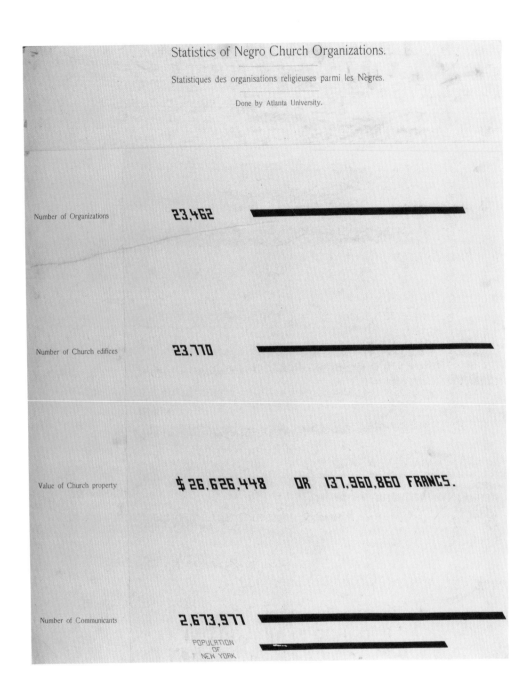

Statistics of Negro Church Organizations.

Statistiques des organisations religieuses parmi les Nègres.

Done by Atlanta University.

Number of Organizations   23,462

Number of Church edifices   23,770

Value of Church property $ 26,626,448   OR 137,960,860 FRANCS.

Number of Communicants   2,673,977

POPULATION
OF
NEW YORK

Plate 63 This bar chart with peculiar typographic
and graphic details presents deeper information
about religious organizations in black communities.
The numerals counting the total number of organizations, church edifices, value of church property,
and number of participants are typeset in a backslant
italics similar to but with bolder weight than the
engineered template (see also plate 60).[33]

Notes

INTRODUCTION

1 W. E. B. Du Bois, "The Princess Steel," ed. Adrienne Brown and Britt Rusert, *PMLA* 130.3 (May 2015): 823–24.

2 On the Du Bois–Atlanta School of Sociology, see Aldon Morris, *The Scholar Denied: W. E. B. Du Bois and the Birth of Modern Sociology* (Berkeley: University of California Press, 2015).

3 Eugene F. Provenzo Jr., *W. E. B. Du Bois's Exhibit of American Negroes: African Americans at the Beginning of the Twentieth Century* (Lanham, MD: Rowan & Littlefield, 2013), 90.

4 David Levering Lewis, "A Small Nation of People: W. E. B. Du Bois and Black Americans at the Turn of the Twentieth Century," in *A Small Nation of People: W. E. B. Du Bois & African American Portraits of Progress*, ed. Library of Congress (New York: Amistad, 2003), 28.

5 Mabel O. Wilson, *Negro Building: Black Americans in the World of Fairs and Museums* (Berkeley: University of California Press, 2012); Library of Congress, *A Small Nation of People*; Shawn Michelle Smith, *Photography on the Color Line: W. E. B. Du Bois, Race, and Visual Culture* (Durham, NC: Duke University Press, 2004); Provenzo, *W. E. B. Du Bois's Exhibit*.

6 *Soul of a Nation: Art in the Age of Black Power*, ed. Mark Godfrey and Zoe Whitley (London: Tate Modern, 2017).

7 "The Surprising History of the Infographic," *Smithsonian*, July 2016; Michael Soto, *Measuring the Harlem Renaissance: The US Census, African American Identity, and Literary Form* (Amherst: University of Massachusetts Press, 2016).

8 "The Negro in Business," *Atlanta University Publications* (New York: Arno Press and the *New York Times*, 1968), 4–5; several women are listed among the investigators in "A Study of Negro City Life: Appendix A," *Atlanta University Publications*, 73.

9 Smith, *Photography on the Color Line*.

10 Du Bois, *The Souls of Black Folk* (New York: Penguin, 1996), 5.

11 Deborah Willis, "The Sociologist's Eye: W. E. B. Du Bois and the Paris Exposition," in *A Small Nation of People*, 67.

12 Du Bois, *The Autobiography of W. E. B. Du Bois: A Soliloquy on Viewing My Life from the Last Decade of Its First Century* (New York: Oxford University Press, 2014), 140–41.

13 Morris, *The Scholar Denied*.

14 Du Bois, *The Souls of Black Folk*, 1.

15 Du Bois, *Autobiography*, 141.

16 *Bulletin of Atlanta University*, 110 (1900): 3. Horace Bumstead Papers, Atlanta University Center, Robert W. Woodruff Library, Atlanta, GA.

17 Thomas J. Calloway to W. E. B. Du Bois, 18 January 1909, W. E. B. Du Bois Papers, Special Collections and University Archives, University of Massachusetts Amherst Libraries.

18 "How Is Digital Mapping Changing the Way We Visualize Racism and Segregation?" *Forbes*, October 20, 2017; Data for Black Lives Conference, MIT Media Lab, November 17–19, 2017.

AMERICAN NEGRO AT PARIS, 1900

1 1900 Exposition Gold Medal Award, ca. August 1900. W. E. B. Du Bois Papers, Special Collections and University Archives, University of Massachusetts Amherst Libraries.

2 Aldon Morris, *The Scholar Denied: W. E. B. Du Bois and the Birth of Modern Sociology* (Berkeley: University of California Press, 2015).

3 Du Bois, "The American Negro at Paris," *American Review of Reviews* (November 1900): 577.

4 Thomas Calloway, "The Negro Exhibit," in *Report of the Commissioner-General for the United States to the International Universal Exposition, Paris, 1900*, vol. II (Washington, DC: Government Printing Office, 1901), 463–67.

5 Calloway, 463–67.

6 W. E. B. Du Bois, *The Souls of Black Folk*, ed. Henry Louis Gates (1903; Oxford: Oxford University Press, 2007).

7   W. E. B. Du Bois, "The Early Beginnings of the Pan-African Movement," 20 June 1958. W. E. B. Du Bois Papers (MS 312), Special Collections and University Archives, University of Massachusetts Amherst Libraries.

8   Frederick L. Hoffman, *Race Traits and Tendencies of the American Negro*, Publications of the American Economic Association, vol. xi, no. 1–3 (New York: Macmillan, 1896).

9   William Wordsworth, "Composed Upon Westminster Bridge, September 3, 1802."

10 Du Bois, "The American Negro," 577.

11 Du Bois, 577.

12 Du Bois, *The Negro Artisan: A Social Study* (Atlanta: Atlanta University Press, 1902), 187.

THE CARTOGRAPHY OF
W. E. B. DU BOIS'S COLOR LINE

1   W. E. B. Du Bois, "To the Nations of the World," Pan-African Congress, London, ca. 1900. W. E. B. Du Bois Papers, Special Collections and University Archives, University of Massachusetts Amherst Libraries.

2   Timothy Mitchell, *Colonising Egypt* (Berkeley: University of California Press, 1991), 28.

3   Mabel O. Wilson, *Negro Building: Black Americans in the World of Fairs and Museums*, (Berkeley: University of California Press, 2012), 97–98.

4   Denis Cosgrove, *Apollo's Eye: A Cartographic Genealogy of the Earth in the Western Imagination* (Baltimore: Johns Hopkins University Press, 2001), 215.

5   W. E. B. Du Bois, "The American Negro at Paris," *American Review of Reviews* (November 1900): 577.

6   Georg Wilhelm Friedrich Hegel, excerpt from "Philosophy of History," in *Race and the Enlightenment: A Reader*, ed. Emmanuel Chukwudi Eze (London: Blackwell, 1997), 142.

7   Hegel, 142.

8   Du Bois, "The American Negro," 577.

9   Du Bois, 577.

PLATES INTRODUCTION & CAPTIONS

1   Mabel O. Wilson, *Negro Building: Black Americans in the World of Fairs and Museums* (Berkeley: University of California Press, 2012), 98.

2   Morris Lewis, "Paris and the International Exposition," *Colored American* (October 1900): 295.

3   Marie Neurath, and Robin Kinross, *The Transformer: Principles of Making Isotype Charts* (London: Hyphen, 2009); Katherine McCoy, "Education in an Adolescent Profession," in *The Education of a Designer*, ed. Steven Heller (New York: Allworth Press, 1998), 3–12; Edward Tufte, *The Visual Display of Quantitative Information* (Cheshire, CT: Graphics Press, 2001).

4   Scott Christianson, *100 Diagrams that Changed the World* (New York: Plume, 2012), 120–23.

5   Christianson, 143.

6   *Bulletin of Atlanta University*, 110 (1900): 3; Shawn Michelle Smith, *Photography on the Color Line: W. E. B. Du Bois, Race, and Visual Culture* (Durham, NC: Duke University Press, 2004), 162.

7   Thomas J. Calloway, "The Negro Exhibit," in *Report of the Commissioner-General for the United States to the International Universal Exposition, Paris, 1900*, vol. II (Washington, DC: Government Printing Office, 1901), 463–67.

8   Because of their fragility, the images are archived at the Library of Congress in window mats. Some reproductions show the actual ragged edges of these timeworn documents, while others have a distinct edge because of the mat in which they were photographed.

9   "Progressive Disclosure," Nielsen Norman Group, accessed October 1, 2017, https://www.nngroup.com/articles/progressive-disclosure/.

10 Lorraine Wild, "Europeans in America," in *Graphic Design in America*, ed. Mildred

Friedman (Minneapolis: Walker Art Center; New York: Abrams, 1989); McCoy, "Education in an Adolescent Profession"; "Teaching and Learning," *Collected Writings of Rob Roy Kelly*, accessed October 1, 2017, http://www.rit.edu/library/archives/rkelly/resources/pdf/03_ped/ped_tea.pdf.

11 Leland Wilkinson and Michael Friendly, "The History of the Cluster Heat Map," *American Statistician* 63.2 (2009): 179–84.

12 "Stylographic Pens," *Vintage Pens*, accessed November 20, 2017, http://www.vintagepens.com/stylos.shtml.

13 Because of the sheer number of letters, the designers could also have made use of a pantograph. A pantograph is a parallelogram-shaped mechanical device that was employed in the nineteenth and twentieth centuries to copy preset letter styles. Pantographs were also engaged in the manufacture of wood type that was parallel to these works. See Rob Roy Kelly, *American Wood Type, 1828–1900: Notes on the Evolution of Decorated and Large Types and Comments on Related Trades of the Period* (1969; Saratoga, CA: Liber Apertus, 2010), 196.

14 Alice Walker, "If the Present Looks Like the Past, What Does the Future Look Like?" (1982), in *In Search of Our Mothers' Gardens* (New York: Mariner Books, 1983), 290–91.

15 Neurath and Kinross, *The Transformer*.

16 Magdalena Droste and Karl Schawelka, *Vassily Kandinsky: Teaching at the Bauhaus* (Berlin: Bauhaus-Archiv Museum für Gestaltung, 2014), 32–36.

17 Christianson, *100 Diagrams*, 143

18 The circle chart as a data form was actually pioneered by William Playfair in his 1801 *Statistical Breviary*; Tufte, *The Visual Display*, 44.

19 Wilson, *Negro Building*, 98.

20 The class levels were determined by Du Bois and are related to his well-known idea of the "Talented Tenth." See Booker T. Washington et al., *The Negro Problem: A Series of Articles by Representative American Negroes of Today* (New York: James Pott and Company, 1903).

21 "Montgomery's Raids in Florida, Georgia, and South Carolina, by William Lee Apthorp, Lt. Colonel, 34th United States Colored Infantry, June 1864," accessed December 29, 2017, http://www.unf.edu/floridahistoryonline/montgomery/; Buddy Sullivan, *Early Days on the Georgia

Tidewater: The Story of McIntosh County and Sapelo*, 4th ed. (Darien, GA: McIntosh County Board of Commissioners, 1990).

22 See note 8.

23 W. E. B. Du Bois, *The Suppression of the African Slave-Trade to the United States of America* (1896; New York: Longmans, Green, and Co., 1904).

24 G. P. Kellaway, *Map Projections* (London: Methuen & Co. Ltd., 1946), 37–38.

25 "New Flag for Afro-Americans," *Africa Times and Orient Review* 1 (October 1912): 134, in *Race First: The Ideological and Organizational Struggles of Marcus Garvey and the Universal Negro Improvement Association* (Westport, CT: Greenwood Press, 1987), 43; George McGuire, *Universal Negro Catechism: A Course of Instruction in Religious and Historical Knowledge Pertaining to the Race.* (New York: Universal Negro Improvement Association, 1921), 34.

26 Tony Martin, *Pan-African Connection: From Slavery to Garvey and Beyond* (Dover: Majority Press, 1985), 207.

27 Robert Bringhurst, *The Elements of Typographic Style* (Seattle: Hartley & Marks, 2016), 122–25.

28 Bringhurst, 93.

29 Clay Shirky, "Power Laws, Weblogs, and Inequality," *Writings About the Internet*, accessed November, 1, 2017, http://www.shirky.com/writings/herecomeseverybody/powerlaw_weblog.html.

30 Peter Irons, "Jim Crow's Schools," *American Educator*, accessed January, 31, 2018, https://www.aft.org/periodical/american-educator/summer-2004/jim-crows-schools.

31 Catherine Cooke, *Russian Avant-Garde: Theories of Art, Architecture and the City* (London: Academy Editions, 1995), 106; Whitney Museum of American Art, Donna M. De Salvo, and Ann Goldstein, *Lawrence Weiner: As Far as the Eye Can See* (Los Angeles: Museum of Contemporary Arts, 2007).

32 William E. Ryan and Theodore E. Conover, *Graphic Communications Today* (Clifton Park, NY: Thomson, 2004), 98.

33 "Nitro & Turbo Overview," Hoefler & Co., accessed November 20, 2017, https://www.typography.com/fonts/nitro-turbo/overview/.

About the Contributors

Whitney Battle-Baptiste is an associate professor in the Department of Anthropology and director of the W. E. B. Du Bois Center at the University of Massachusetts Amherst. A native of the Bronx, New York, and a member of the Hip-Hop generation, she is a scholar and activist who sees the classroom and the campus as spaces to engage contemporary issues with a sensibility of the past. Her work actively uses the tools of archaeology to interpret the landscapes of captivity and freedom, and she has led excavations on a variety of archaeo-logical sites. Her current project incorporates geospatial analysis into a community-based heritage site project at Millars Plantation on the island of Eleuthera in the Bahamas. Her first book, *Black Feminist Archaeology* (Left Coast Press, 2011), outlines the basic tenets of Black Feminist thought as a method for enhancing archaeological theory and practice.

Aldon Morris is the Leon Forrest Professor of Sociology and African American Studies at Northwestern University. He has published widely on social movements, race, religion, social inequality, and the sociology of W. E. B. Du Bois. He is the author of *The Origins of the Civil Rights Movement* (Free Press, 1984), which won the 1986 Distinguished Contribution to Scholarship Award from the American

Sociological Association, and co-editor of the volumes *Frontiers in Social Movement Theory* (Yale, 1992) and *Opposition Consciousness: The Subjective Roots of Social Protest* (University of Chicago, 2001). Most recently he authored the award-winning book *The Scholar Denied: W. E. B. Du Bois and the Birth of Modern Sociology* (University of California, 2015). In 2009 Morris won the Cox-Johnson-Frazier Award from the American Sociological Association for a lifetime of research, scholarship, and teaching.

Silas Munro is an educator and designer who applies design to inspire people to elevate themselves and improve society. His Los Angeles–based studio, Poly-Mode, helps organizations embrace cultural diversity and increase community involvement. His studio has collaborated with MoMA, the Baltimore Museum of Art, Mark Bradford, and Miami's Wynwood Arts District, among others. Munro's design work and writings have been published in many forms at home and abroad. As an educator, he focuses on expanded design studies. He has been a critic, lecturer, and professor at many internationally ranked art and design programs. Munro is an assistant professor at Otis College of Art and Design and an advisor at Vermont College of Fine Arts.

Britt Rusert is an interdisciplinary scholar whose research is situated at the intersections of race and science, Afrofuturism, gender and sexuality studies, and visual culture. She is the author of *Fugitive Science: Empiricism and Freedom in Early African American Culture* (New York University, 2017) and an assistant professor in the W. E. B. Du Bois Department of Afro-American Studies at the University of Massachusetts Amherst. She is currently at work on two projects: *The Fantasy Worlds of W. E. B. Du Bois*, a collection of Du Bois's short

genre fiction co-edited with Adrienne Brown; and a monograph about William J. Wilson's *Afric-American Picture Gallery* (1859), a text that imagines the first museum of black art in the United States.

Mabel O. Wilson is an architectural designer and cultural historian. She is the author of *Begin with the Past: Building the National Museum of African American History and Culture* (Smithsonian, 2016) and *Negro Building: African Americans in the World of Fairs and Museums* (University of California, 2012). At Columbia University she is a professor of architecture, a co-director of Global Africa Lab, and associate director of the Institute for Research in African American Studies.

Acknowledgments

The editors wish to thank the Library of Congress Prints and Photographs Division for permission to reproduce images from the Daniel Murray collection; the University of Massachusetts Amherst Special Collections and University Archives for permission to reproduce material from the W. E. B. Du Bois Papers; Tiffany Atwater and the graduate student staff of the Archives Research Center at the Atlanta University Center Woodruff Library for assistance with archival documents; Eugene F. Provenzo Jr., David Levering Lewis, John H. Bracey Jr., Lauren Klein, Ruha Benjamin, Robert Paynter, and Lana Dever. At the University of Massachusetts Amherst: Carol Connare, Simon Neame, Rob Cox, and Danielle Kovacs of the UMass Amherst Libraries; the W. E. B. Du Bois Department of Afro-American Studies; the students in Britt Rusert's fall 2017 Du Bois Senior Seminar. At Princeton Architectural Press: Nina Pick, Nolan Boomer, Abby Bussel, Ben English, and Susan Hershberg. Aldon Morris would like to thank the editors for their valuable comments on his essay. Silas Munro thanks Stephen Munro, Ian Lynam, and Stan Kaplan, as well as the Vermont College of Fine Arts and Virginia Commonwealth University School of the Arts for support of early presentations of this research.

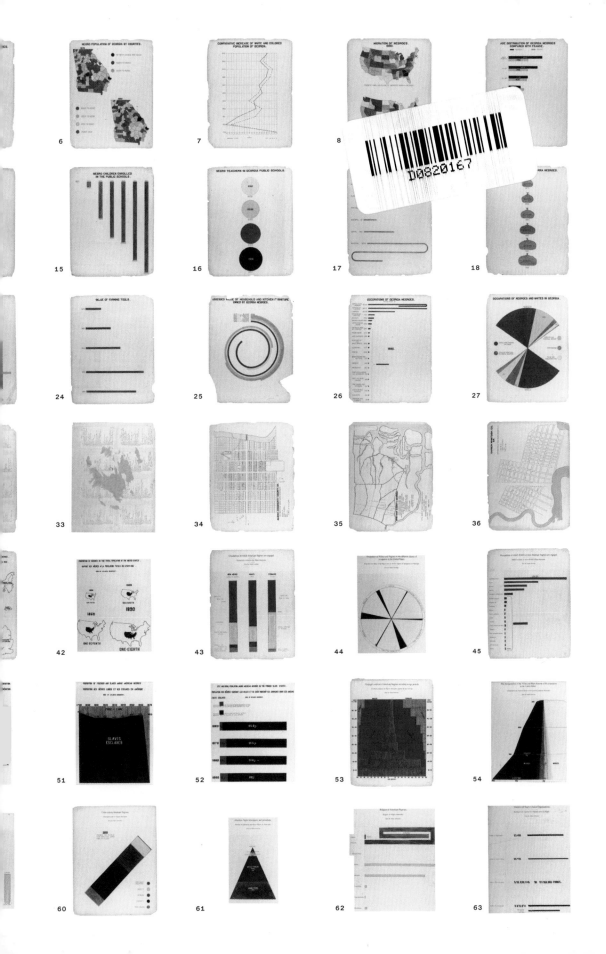